THE ELECT

The Elect

William J. McDonald

Exposition Press   Hicksville, New York

Contents

Preface

Shakespeare said: "Life's but a walking shadow, a poor player that struts and frets his hour upon the stage and then is heard no more: it is a tale told by an idiot, full of sound and fury, signifying nothing."

That sentiment—that life is a meaningless drama ending in death—is being embraced by much of the world today—but needlessly. The seemingly unconnected troubles of life can be explained by a few principles, which apply to them all.

If a man who was born blind were to ask you to describe red, yellow and blue, what would you tell him? You would be mistaken, if you said, "I cannot explain; you would have to see for yourself."

This book will prove there is a close relationship between the causes of many sensory phenomena—such as color, feelings, and tastes, such as sour, sweet, bitter and salt—and spiritual things. Spiritual things, of course, are the most important, but all phenomena are explainable by the same laws. It was the discovery of truth in its spiritual form that resulted in the writing of this book.

When spiritual truth is well understood, it is possible to take any problem and discover the answer by spiritual means alone, whether that problem be mechanical, political or philosophical.

For this reason—the interrelatedness of all things—this book offers knowledge that can help ensure eternal life. Questions such as What do atoms and molecules look like? How were they created? can be explained here, because the answer has such a close relationship to the main theme of this book.

It is hard to tell which kind of problem will hold the most

interest to the average person, and which answers are the most sought after. There was the man who argued that he could see no possible reason why the crucifixion of someone else should help him in any way. No proof was asked for, only a possible explanation of relevance. The Bible asks you to believe without an explanation. But we need a substantial explanation for all the suffering in the world.

My hope is that each reader will find some answers for himself in the following pages.

WJM

THE ELECT

1

What Feelings Are

This book is not fiction or fantasy. It deals with a group of real people who form a team. They do not, however, all live in the world at the same time. But they are—and so are called—The Elect. They make their presence known to us in many ways.

A boy of thirteen named Forest Crook told me of an experience he had at school that puzzled him very much. Standing in front of his class, the boy suddenly saw a man a few feet away, though Forest knew that the man was appearing only in his mind. The man was large, blond and Swedish-looking. The boy asked, "Who are you?"

The man replied, "Axel Nelson," then disappeared.

While already very young, Forest had noticed that some people talked and acted much smarter than others. He adopted this idea of "smartness" as an ideal and wanted to do and say everything as elegantly as possible.

In the schoolroom debate, Forest thought he saw a clever way to present his side of the case. Yet after he began talking he realized he had overlooked something in the preparation of his rhetoric and that as a result of this oversight his argument would seem stupid. This created a very strong feeling within him which transcended the limits of his mind.

Such an experience—that of contact on another plane—is not as uncommon as might be supposed. I have heard my father tell a story of when he was a boy in Arkansas, before 1870. He and his two older brothers would go ghost-hunting at night with some other boys. My dad was the youngest of the lot, but when one of them would point into the woods and say, "There's a ghost!" he could always keep up with the rest in scampering for safety.

One night the gang played a joke on my father. They had him stand in a clearing and watch, while they dispersed. The boys were supposed to come back to the clearing, but instead they all hid in the blackness and remained quiet.

My father told me that he became more frightened than at any time in his life—until suddenly he saw someone standing beside him. He could tell that the one he saw was in his own mind. The fellow's low-bridge nose and lankiness were very clear to him. He was not a figment of imagination; he was one of the Elect, who responded to my father's desire to escape.

There are many cases of people who display distinctly different personalities at different times. Until I was twenty-six years old, I could have argued honestly that I had never known such a person; then I realized that I myself had this trait. I began to remember a certain ability I had had all my life. I could "lift" my memory so that it caused no interference when aiming at the Spirit of Truth. With my memory out of the way, I could know anything I wanted. The higher I lifted my memory, the easier it became to discover the truth about any subject, no matter how complicated.

I could grasp anything, but these truths didn't go into my memory, and when I set my memory down again, the facts were not in it, except in some vague high-level way, of which I was not normally conscious. When talking with others about this mind shifting, I would call the two states "being smart" and "being dumb."

A boy once asked, "How would it be if you would get smart and tell me things, and when you get dumb I'll tell them back to you?" I told him that his teaching them back to me would make me smart as soon as he began speaking, and when I got dumb again I still would not know them. So, I normally avoided using this ability. Actually, I was aiming at the truth to a small degree at all times, and for the sole purpose of determining whether or not to lift my memory further.

Then, when I was twenty-five years old, and with my memory firmly in place, and after much contemplation, I figured out the causes of pride and happiness. I discovered also, that the truth about any subject has a feeling connected to it.

I had spent quite some time trying to figure out what Emmanuel meant in the Bible when he said that he was the Truth. Once I figured it out, I felt a deep-seated happiness that became so strong I would wake up in the morning with the memory of feeling elated all night. It made me recall feeling that way when I was three years old. I also learned that happiness is open to anyone who seeks the truth, and that the strength of the feeling is proportional to the strength of the desire.

One thing my happiness did was cause me to remember everything that previously I could not remember at all. I remembered all the facts I had been able to explain at an early age when I could lift my memories anytime the Spirit of Truth was willing. Among other things, I could remember how feelings, colors and tastes were created; what is necessary to live forever; how eternity will seem to those who find it; how atoms were made and how they look; and the causes of homosexuality.

When I now set out to learn something, such as how atoms behave, it feels as though I am chinning myself on the problem and hanging there until the answer soaks through, sometimes hours or days later.

My present way of finding answers enables me to understand seemingly supernatural occurrences. For instance, when I was examining a gun, my carelessness resulted in it firing a bullet into the wall. A few years later, my uncle, who lived in another state, came on a visit. While we were discussing gun accidents, he asked to see the bullet hole and said he would tell me what kind of gun had fired the bullet. He was able to do this exactly but could never explain how he did it. It was several years before I understood how he could know all about a gun without seeing it, and I understood only when I had found answers to much more fundamental questions about feelings in general.

Feelings, I learned, are important not only as the cause of events but as the ultimate goal of history, next to life itself in importance.

If you take a few assorted responses such as pride, excitement, pain, fear, and happiness and consider each one very deeply, they will begin to stand out like a row of objects, and be revealed as units of a vast puzzle. People with certain mental illnesses may change emotionally from one extreme to the other, with no change in their environment. This shows that feelings are caused by more than external circumstances alone. The problem is to discover what are feelings made of.

For this we need to realize that an instinct is nothing but memory inherited from a long line of ancestors. In this book, at least, that is what the word *instinct* will always be used to mean. Instincts play such an important part in the creation and operation of this universe that some evidence to help prove their nature might be in order.

Our ancestors ran into caves to save their lives and rolled large boulders into the mouths of the caves behind them, just ahead of some animal with long claws. When the animal arrived and tried to claw the rocks out of the way, it made a scraping sound like that of your fingernails along slate. When you hear such a sound now, it brings to the surface the memory of those ancient happenings. You get a cold, shivery feeling up your back —as if you had just made it safely into your cave!

The lower the form of animal life, the more the animal depends on its instinct. A spider, for example, is an astonishingly able engineer. Yet, the spider does not have to figure out how to build its web, nor could it.

Every one of us has ancestors who nearly starved to death, as well as endured all kinds of trouble. Everything that happens to us, in later generations is compared to all of our past knowledge and experiences, and also to our inherited knowledge. If our ancestors had as easy a time getting something to eat as they did getting a drink of water, we now would get no more enjoyment from eating than we do from drinking water. But our ancestors did get dehydrated enough that it now makes our pleasure greater to drink water when *we* are truly thirsty. We have inherited their memories of the same pleasure, which also increases our own pleasure.

Our ancestors had no trouble getting fresh air, so breathing fresh air brings no similar pleasure.

Young children a few years old are easier to make happy than anyone else. Although they don't have much acquired knowledge, they are much closer to their own inherited knowledge. This makes for a stronger comparison between instinct and experience. At that age everything that is good seems better, everything that is bad seems worse. In later life accumulated memories insulate us from such a strong comparison.

Stronger memories are inherited from each parent than from each grandparent, but since there are twice as many grandparents, the sum total of their memories may be more. If all your ancestors had been perfectly happy all the time, then even though you were also happy, you would not appreciate it. If someone told you that what you felt was called happiness, you would call happiness a neutral feeling. It was necessary for your ancestors to have had considerable pain, misery, trouble, and woe—and for you to have inherited a memory of it—to make your experiences seem good and reassuring by comparison.

All of our memories and inherited memories put together are what the Bible calls the heart of man, so that each thought and each experience that happens to a person are compared to his own Heart of Man. Your Heart of Man is a middle-of-the-road fellow, the average of all feelings, your normal self. Anything better than this seems good; anything worse seems bad. This is the principle behind all enjoyment and misery.

If we did everything our Heart of Man makes us want to do, we would do many good things, for we had many ancestors who wanted to do good things. But this is also what caused its deceitfulness, for no ancestor was perfect. In Jer.17:9 it is said, "The heart is deceitful above all things, and desperately wicked." For this reason it cannot be used forever as a comparison for thoughts and experiences.

When living forever is mentioned, some will say, "You live only once." Well, if you live forever, you live only once.

We are living in this world now to make feelings better for eternity. It has taken so much misery in the world to build up feelings, generation after generation, that any way to make feelings stronger is desirable. And there is a very good way. It has been in use since human feelings began. Suppose you have a thought, desire, or experience. When it is compared to your

Heart of Man, it is like being conscious of both it and the Heart of Man at the same time; the comparison is the feeling. But there is a way to make feelings even stronger.

For example: if you are in a situation from which you wish to escape, the thought of trying to get away, when compared to the Heart of Man, creates the feeling of fear. If you could then suddenly know all the situations in the world where anyone has ever tried to escape from danger, this additional knowledge compared to your Heart of Man would create much stronger feelings. That is exactly what does happen; but this knowledge must be brought into your mind for you to have it.

If you could feel fear strong enough in relation to your inherited memories of this feeling, your fear would then change from an emotion and would take on the substantiality of a person you could recognize, if you knew him.

That is what happened in my father's case, and what puzzled him so much when he was a boy out ghost-hunting. He wanted to escape his predicament with a desire so strong that he saw the person who made his fear become so strong.

When this person comes up in your mind, he brings with him the knowledge of each time anyone has ever tried to escape from danger, so that this knowledge is compared with your Heart of Man. The stronger you wish to escape, the further he rises into your consciousness. If he comes far enough, you will actually see him.

Some things make so strong an impression that they are easy to remember. When I was not yet four years old, I was walking on a gravel road about one-half mile from home with older companions. I told them, with great feeling, that we were not getting any place, for I was tired. This feeling became so strong that it became a man at whom I could look, although seeing such a person may change the thought so fast that he will disappear.

When Forest Crook told me that he had seen a man named Axel Nelson in the schoolroom, when no one else could see or hear him, I could very easily lift my Heart of Man out of the way and know anything I wanted to. I asked Forest if he felt "like a fool" just before he saw him. Forest said that he had not realized that the way he felt had anything to do with it.

A few years later, I became acquainted with Axel Nelson in person. He also was brighter than average, with a dignified manner and a strong, persistent sense of humor. This condition often caused him to feel the same way Forest had felt; in fact, Axel could do it easier than anyone else.

It is possible to feel the truth about anything, but this usually appears in a very weak form. Emmanuel is the Spirit of Truth. The feeling for the truth is more like the finding of a way, and the way becomes plainer the more you use it. You pick your way through your personal memories and the inherited ones to find the truth.

When I first discovered that the truth had a feeling I could feel, it seemed like a new and wonderful tool with which to do things. I had never written a poem in my life, yet it seemed like a good means to try out this ability. The following writing took less than an hour to create:

FIRST THINGS FIRST

"Smart" people may say, let us strive for success,
Let us do things to earn fortune and fame.
If we try hard enough and do our best,
In the world of the future we may leave our name.

But some people look and see things all about,
See things they know nothing of
They may laugh or play or cry or shout.
But what is happiness or sadness or love?*

Many have wondered where mysteries are from.
"Give me insight into today," as Emerson said.
The wonder of the future is for generations to come,
And the glories of the past I leave to the dead.

---

*When I wrote this line, I had no idea what they were made of.

Why should steam lift a kettle lid?
Why should an apple fall down?
Men who have found where these mysteries hid
Are the men who have won renown.

Why should a war cause millions to die?
Why should a nation be torn?
Anyone who thinks there is no need to try,
That man was dead before he was born.

No need to turn the world upside down
To find "An eye for an eye, and a tooth for a tooth."
No need for a horse to ride through the town,
But let's discover first how to discover the truth.

To understand how to aim at the truth through all of your memories and inherited memories, it is essential to know what a memory is. Every experience of each moment of your life is continually compared by your mind to all your past memories and instincts; it is this comparison which makes a feeling. A feeling is knowledge compared to knowledge, and your memory is nothing but a memory of this feeling.

If yesterday you saw a car go by and today you remember how it looked, what happened in your mind was that you allowed a memory of a feeling to steer your imagination, while you imagined a mental picture of a car. But there are no sights or sounds in your memory, only the feelings that each moment of your life makes when it is compared with your Heart of Man. To see the past any other way is from a different source than from your ordinary memory.

Anyone with a strong desire for knowledge will, as a result, have a stronger memory. There are methods of associating ideas that are very useful as memory aids, and these should not be overlooked by persons wishing to develop good memories. But persons with naturally strong memories already have a strong desire to learn.

When it comes to learning by spiritual means, it is so difficult to sense the truth through all your other feelings that most people are unable to do so, unless they believe they are approaching death, and often even then they cannot isolate the truth from the random flow of experience.

However, there is an easier way to find true facts, and that is to have another feeling show the way. The truth itself is one feeling, and wanting to know the truth is another. Wanting to know earnestly enough will develop the feeling that can show the way.

When I was ten years old, I went to bed one night deeply engrossed in a problem. I tried to see through it with so much desire that in my mind I saw a boy coming towards me, looking first to one side, then the other. This is the only time I ever tried to see through a problem with so much desire that I saw the one who is the spirit behind it.

This one can aim at the Spirit of Truth to some degree himself. Given enough time and opportunity, he will steer you in the right direction. In other words, if you keep wanting to know the truth about something while you cast about in all directions trying to find it, you will usually find it.

However, most people aim too far ahead and want the *consequences* of discovering the truth, rather than the truth itself. The consequences might include many desirable feelings, as well as money and success.

Many everyday thoughts are caused by instincts. For example, in the early days of commercial trade the buyer would step off, heel to toe, the amount of anything measured by length. Then came the arguing over price. If the buyer's feet were small, he would argue the price down. Each buyer would like to point out that he had small feet. As weak as this instinct is, it still makes people want to brag about their small feet. Usually by wearing shoes that are too tight.

An ideal education should have as its main object teaching us how to think. One very important part of thinking is to *study* the problem. Most people form opinions without taking half enough time to do this. Another part of education is the knowledge of how human minds work, and which way is the best for finding the right answers. That is our quest here.

2

Unique Ways
of Knowing Things

Some things in this book were arrived at backwards—by induction rather than deduction. If a criminal case were solved in this way, the police would first make an arrest, then hunt for evidence to indicate they had the right man. To figure out things my way you have to be able to "make up your mind," quite literally.

Making up your mind in this sense is a form of self-hypnotism. If you make up your mind strong enough to do a certain thing at a certain time, you will, even though you have forgotten about your earlier decision to do it.

To solve problems this way, you make up your mind, by thinking as hard as you can that you want and need the answer to a certain problem. For example: I wanted facts about atomic behavior and how the negative aspects, the failures, the pain, the inequities, fit the master plan of this universe. I would see mental pictures of all kinds of things, with no apparent connection. This at first would seem like daydreaming. The ideas would start out disconnected; but they later would fit together as the explanation. The ideas were too complicated to fit together accidentally—thus providing their own proof.

The main ideas in this book are based on the belief that the future is planned and, therefore, knowable. Many nights during sleep I have seen parts of the future which later always came true. These were not only large events but insignificant ones, too. Some of these I had written down months before they happened. Seeing parts of the future while asleep is usually difficult to remember.

20

Life is planned. Not a word or deed in the future will occur that hasn't happened already in the plans. This present moment is like the point of a phonograph needle. As the record plays, the part yet to come is just as much a reality as the part that has been played. Tomorrow is already there.

Some believe that when your time comes to die, you go, if not from one cause, then from another. However, not only the important events of your life are predestined to happen at a definite time, but *every* detail.

The Bible refers to life in this world as "under the sun." Ecc. 1:9, "There is no new thing under the sun." Each life has built-in trouble, explained by the theory that feelings are knowledge compared to knowledge. Besides being the foundation for feelings, knowledge is so important that better ways of acquiring it should be sought after. The most important knowledge would be of a spiritual nature.

There are different ways of knowing things other than by ordinary reasoning. Only the spiritual ways will be discussed here. Revelation of truth can come to anyone. Discovery is for those who seek it.

Acquiring one method of revelation is possible, because each person plans his own life before he is born. It is possible to stop planning your life at any point and to find out whatever it is you want to know; ask God, if necessary. Then make up your mind that it is that way. This leaves imprints on your mind as definite as sound recorded on a phonograph record.

There are no voices or music on a phonograph record, only ups and downs in the groove. When you think something strong enough, it also leaves imprints on your mind; it is possible to change these imprints back to what caused them. The more important the subject, and therefore the higher the concentration, the easier it is to do. Yet most people have too much interference from other feelings, except when they are very young, to do this well, or to interpret real truth from mere sensation.

Another way to know things is to use your memory at the time you spiritually enter this world, which is not until you take your first breath of air. Using your memory at that time will form a track you can use later to remember things you knew before you were born. Doing so will change your looks slightly, causing a purple shade to the color of your eyes.

Another way is to aim at the truth by backing away from the feeling of pride. I have known several people who could do this. One boy had never felt proud in his life, except once. He used this one experience as if it were a lighthouse, then backed away from it. Another boy had tried to feel proud so many times that in learning to pull on this feeling he also learned how to push against it. If a person could go all the way in backing away from pride, he would be where Emmanuel is, and could see everything in a bright light of pure truth.

Few have ever gone over ten percent of the way towards this light, but this is enough to know almost anything, like looking at it through a fog. It will still not work for a selfish motive, nor if you want the answer to be satisfactory to you stronger than you want to know which way it is.

Another way to aim at the truth is by going forward into the future. That is the source of most of the ideas in this book. Either way leads through the plans of your life; both go in a complete circle and come back to the present.

To back up against the Spirit of Truth is to back away from this world. There are no feelings in backing up against the Spirit of Truth, and anyone who can do it has that ability as a spiritual gift. You cannot demonstrate this ability so that it will change anyone's religious belief fundamentally.

The reason why the ones who back up against the Spirit of Truth keep it virtually a secret, is that doing it is in the class with miracles. Such miracles are kept secret, because if anyone aimed at the truth well enough to believe that Emmanuel performed the miracles he did, this alone would ensure that he would live forever—but not if he were *forced* to believe it. If someone were to demonstrate miracles, those who witnessed them would get no credit for believing what they saw. If they believed then that Emmanuel *could* do miracles, this would not be enough for them to live forever. He would get no credit for believing what his *senses* made him believe. Therefore, it would be even more difficult for him to be able to live forever than it was before.

While backing up against the truth is a gift, going forward is a skill. Anyone can do this, and the better he learns how, the happier a feeling he will derive from the experience.

The happier you feel, the nearer to the front of your mind a certain person comes. Yet, the state of mind we call happiness is nothing but a closer association with the Spirit of Truth through the Heart of Man. An example will show why.

There was a goat-hoofed fellow named Pan, and others of that ilk, who were actually made out of nothing, even though they scared people to death. Ever since the Spirit of Truth came to live in this world, they could no longer exist. But since that time, as well as before, there have been human beings who have "gone off the deep end." There have been vampires, werewolves, warlocks, witches and many more variants of normal human nature. How these came about could be explained; but explained or not, they are still in man's inherited memories, as well as are all kinds of crime and misery. Anything that will cause a closer association with the Spirit of Truth through this evil will cause a more enjoyable feeling than any other. This is happiness, which can be of any strength or intensity, from a bland sense of rightness to an overwhelming joy.

There are many pleasurable feelings besides happiness. Some people may feel much pride and other kinds of pleasure, like all of it, yet still derive no feeling of happiness from it.

There are other ways of getting happiness besides using skills. For instance, the stronger you want something, the happier you will feel when you get it. This includes anything that creates a desire. If you have a strong desire to get rid of some terrible misery, then getting rid of it will create happiness. If you had never known misery, its absence would cause no happiness.

It is a well-known medical fact that happiness will help patients recover from many physical ailments. Most cancer is susceptible to cure through happiness in relation to a kind of ambition or energy. An unorganized or runaway growth of cells is prevented by a closer association with the Spirit of Truth.

A case in point is that of a naval officer who was found to have cancer that had progressed too far for treatment. He was promoted to captain, since he was not long for this world. Twenty years later an operation was performed for something else. It was then found that his cancer had healed.

There are ways of making up your mind that will cause happiness automatically under certain conditions. For example, when you were very young you might have seen an expanse of blue sky and associated this with a particularly happy thought, an association strong enough to stay with you the rest of your life. The happy thought might have been glider flying in ages to come. And this knowledge acquired by aiming at the truth.

A happy thought is anything that makes a comparison between the Heart of Man and the Spirit of Truth. It could be argued that the comparison is made with God, that the Spirit of Truth is only the way to God. When one goes through his own instincts to reach God, it is like emerging into some place where you have a strong desire to be, even though you go only a short way. But the principle is the same, and in adult life when you see an area of blue sky framed in like-appearing clouds, you may again feel happiness automatically, without remembering its cause.

God told a girl to make up her mind that it was good for her to like to play baseball, because a certain fellow liked it, then not to think any more about it. The fellow in the case was someone she wanted to marry more than she wanted anything else. She wondered later why she got so much happiness out of playing ball.

The way to get the most happiness from any game of skill is to try as hard as you can to make each play perfect; trying to win as though your life depended on it, while, at the same time, you feel there is no penalty on losing, as though it didn't matter. These two feelings are difficult to have at the same time, but if all the players thought this way they would play till the sun went down, even though they forgot the score by the third inning; it would be that much fun.

In any game requiring skill, the more skill you use the more fun you get. To acquire skill rapidly, learn to aim at the Spirit of Truth instead of your own satisfaction. As an example: suppose you have a certain amount of money and wish to ride as far as you can on the bus. You are also hungry and need better clothes. You may spend some money on yourself, or ride as far as you can. Likewise, when a ballplayer steps up to the plate, he has only a certain amount of desire to spend. If he spends it all in wanting to hit the ball, he will try with as much skill as he has at the moment, and will be on the track to acquire more skill rapidly. However, if he desires to impress others, or get pleasure, or win the ballgame, he will be spending his desire on himself, and will not go far as a ballplayer.

Whatever you do, say, or think, there are only two ways to aim. One is to aim at yourself (your own feelings and wants), the other is to aim at truth. To aim at the truth perfectly, you have to deny yourself completely.

But usually it is the Heart of Man that makes you want what you want. Emmanuel says, "I am the way, the truth, and the life: no man comes to the Father but by me" (John 14:6).

The sentence in the Bible that impressed me more than any other was the question asked by Pilate, "What is truth?" That rang a bell. The dictionary defines *truth* as "agreement with fact." But the ability to discover the truth has a feeling connected with it; it needed investigating. I later found out that discovering the truth about the truth can cause happiness.

The main thing in finding out the truth by going forward is to want to know the truth with a desire strong enough so that it creates a feeling; then to use this feeling to steer your way along in your own imagination. This is much like threading your way through a jungle, which makes it subject to error, for it is difficult to keep out other feelings which flock in by association. The easiest way to fool yourself is to look first to see which way you want the answer to come out, then to look for evidence to prove it is that way.

When a person speaks, he has thousands of words in his memory; yet the right ones pop out automatically, in the proper sequence. This is really a trial-and-error method of finding the right word, but all words are tried simultaneously. Everything, even this universe, was created by trial-and-error.

That which makes the right word fall into place can be seen by some when they are very young. I heard a boy of three ask, "What is that so bright I can see?" After trying to figure it out while he was still looking at it he added, "Is that what makes the words come out? Yes, that's what makes the words come out." After that he went into another room to tell his mother that he knew what made the words come out. But when he came back and tried to figure out more, it puzzled him and he said, "Well, how does it work? Now this is not *me* talking! Well, how does it work, anyway?"

The explanation for the foregoing is that the boy was much closer than average to the Spirit of Truth, and could see a spiritual light. Also, at his age there was not yet too much interference caused by memories.

Even though *you* don't see all the words in your mind, in order to pick out the right ones, something does, and that something is the Spirit of Truth. Some people are standing closer to the spiritual light than others and can tell more easily what the Spirit of Truth sees.

This closeness to the Spirit of Truth is a very special part of intelligence, which most people notice but seldom understand. It is usually spoken of as smartness. The reason smartness tends to be colloquial is that people intuitively use the right word in speaking of that part of intelligence that remains constant all during life. The closer you stand to the light the more smartness you have.

Emmanuel has a task that makes it necessary for him to be smarter than anyone else, for the same reason that you would need to be able to run faster than any runner you were holding a light for, when you run in front of him on a dark night.

Whenever you try to think of a new idea or the solution to a problem, the Spirit of Truth looks at it first. This knowledge is compared with your own total knowledge and causes a very weak feeling. But if you are able to change this feeling into the knowledge that caused it, you will have the solution. This will make for a degree of happiness you will then become aware of, depending on how much desire you had to know it.

Any kind of skill requires the ability to aim at the truth,

whether it is a game of skill, mastering a musical instrument, inventing things, or formulating a philosophy such as in this book. If it is done for the right motive, it will cause happiness. The motive that interferes with happiness the most is pride, especially in developing a skill. Whether one becomes a good inventor or not, for example, depends almost entirely upon how much enjoyment one gets out of it. Each one of us should become an inventor. There are rules that can help us do so.

In addition to smartness and knowledge, which are not as important as they sound, inventive ability can be greatly improved by learning four rules: First, everything is invented on a trial-and-error principle. You need to know this so you won't try to invent something as if by magic. Second, you should eliminate most of the mistakes first without building the invention in order to find them. Not appreciating this has caused many inventions to be built before they were half thought out. A third rule is to make all knowledge stand on the evidence that indicates it is so. A tendency to feel that you know something is a handicap. The fourth rule is that any test of your invention must be done for two reasons, to prove that it is right and to prove that it is wrong. When you are testing, look for what is wrong just as much as you look for what is right.

A person may derive enough fun from inventing that he spends more time doing it. And because he spends more time inventing, he acquires more skill. And because of more skill, he gets more fun than he did before. He now spends even more time, develops more skill and gets more enjoyment. Nothing succeeds like success.

The word *intelligence* includes all of your mental faculties, especially knowledge. Your intelligence on any subject can increase, but your distance from the Spirit of Truth remains the same all of your life. I will call this distance smartness. You were born with the amount of smartness you have today. Every time you use it, you have the choice of which way to aim it.

When you begin a speech, if your basic desire is to not say the wrong thing, you may have no desire left over to desire the right thing. You need a positive goal instead of a negative one. And you need to aim at the object that needs explaining instead of at yourself. The Spirit of Truth can give you what you want but you must want it first.

When you want your arm to move, it moves, but all you did to cause the movement was to *want* it to move. You don't move your arm muscles any more than you make your heart beat. You have an inherited faith that when you want your muscles to move, they will. But it is the Spirit of Truth that accomplishes it.

In the human family the difference between involuntary muscles, such as heart muscles, and voluntary muscles, which comprise most of the musculature of the body, is that you made up your mind before you were born to make your heart beat the way it is supposed to beat.

The trouble with making up your mind is that you can still make it up, to a rather strong degree, *after* you are born, usually until you are several years old. The smarter you are, the easier you can do it. But the amount of smartness needed to accomplish this depends on how much worldly feeling, mostly pride, you have to push out of your mind to get at it. When a person feels an undesirable compulsion because of a past decision, it is possible for him to escape it—if he can remember the time he made the decision, provided the reason for making it is no longer present and operative.

A boy I knew well was told when he was very young to go on a road which he knew, so he would not get lost, as he once had done. He was so fearful of becoming lost that he made his mind up to go always on a road that he knew. When he moved to the other side of town, he was within half a mile of the swimming hole. However, when he went to it, he used a horseshoe-shaped route, avoiding the much easier way. He was ten years old then and was smarter than the average. Not until he remembered the time when he made up his mind was he able to untangle himself from his wasteful compulsion. This made for a strong feeling of freedom. Until then, the decision he had stuck in his mind compelled him to go the old route, even though it made a strong "down in the dumps" feeling to go that way. "And ye shall know the truth, and the truth shall make you free" (John 8:32).

At a very early age many people have had a frustrating experience with machines, and as a result made up their minds that they dislike mechanisms. These people are likely to turn to social activities and be called extroverts.

Some people have formed lifetime decisions that interfere with social activities. Such people are likely to discover the joys of thinking and spend so much time at it they are called introverts. It is possible to fully enjoy both. Also to be inhibited in both.

When you make a decision so strong that it influences your actions in the future, though you have forgotten the original decision, this kind of influence comes from the Spirit of Truth third of your mind. When your ideals influence you, that is from the same part of your mind as your memories and instincts. The Holy Ghost holds ideals, the Spirit of Truth holds decisions, and the Spirit of Love holds commitments.

If you have your mind only ten percent made up to do something, the influence to do it still can be very strong. If you have your mind completely made up to do a thing, then you have to do it, if it's humanly possible. If it's impossible, it will make you feel as though you are scraping your brains over a nutmeg grater. This is not a state of mind but is more physical, like vibrations in your head.

There are people who went to Sunday school when they were young and there learned to believe that God was an old man hidden behind the sky. After they got older and more scientific, they decided there was no God. And they were right, for there is no person like what they had called God. What they now call God is the result of early ideals and decisions.

Another name for God is life. Whether it is a tree, or a grasshopper, or the devil himself, the part that is life is God! "If God be for us, who can be against us?" (Rom. 8:31). An appreciation of that last question makes it possible to look forward with anticipation toward a high degree of happiness. To understand how this world is going to end in complete happiness, it is necessary to understand the plans that were laid for it from the beginning.

3

In the Beginning

Human beings obey laws of behavior as defined and immutable as weight succumbing to the law of gravitation. When you were working out your life plan, you could anticipate what everyone was going to do on this world, except yourself. Likewise, when everyone else planned his life, he could anticipate what you and all the rest were going to do. His own life he had to plan.

When you do whatever you want to at a time when you seem to have a large choice of alternatives, the reason you can be anticipated is that you have to want exactly what you do want.

Your wants are determined by your heredity and your environment, including all past experiences. Your heredity is fixed, and when you change your environment it is because of heredity and past environment. Each time you ever did anything it was caused by these two forces. This goes back to a time when you were so young that you had no voice in the planning of your environment. Therefore, you could be anticipated each step of the way.

The main principle behind these laws which determine human behavior is the fact that when all things are considered, there are never two ways to do a thing in which each is equally right for eternity.

With if's, and's, and but's added, anything might be improved. As an example, "if" you had certain opportunities "and" the right help from others, you could improve eternity "but" for your own shortcomings. When all things are considered, there are no if's, and's, and but's. Everything has to be as it is.

If you have an accident, such as an automobile wreck, the same wreck happened in your plans before you were born. At that time you might have gone back in your plans and changed it if you could have done this without an iota of selfishness, but this would be difficult. The only substitute for selfishness that would allow you to change your plans is a desire to have things right. If the desire is strong enough to eliminate the selfishness, and if you could have found a way to make eternity as good some other way, then you could have changed events so the accident would never have happened. Any such change would have been anticipated by anyone who planned out his life in relation to yours.

This is the best possible world, best in making eternity the best for the most people with the least amount of trouble. This universe was created as if God started with eternity and planned everything backwards to the beginning, then began running the universe forward. Thus assuring a perfect eternity.

Of all the people created since the beginning of time, 664 were created and elected to be the foundation of this universe. They are called *The Elect*. The number of the Elect is 666. Number one of the Elect is God, and number 666 is made out of nothing. He is the "abomination of desolation." All the rest are ordinary-appearing human beings.

Most feelings are personified by someone or something, most of them by the Elect. For the majority of feelings each one has some thought as its beginning. For example, when you think you can build something difficult to build, or finish some difficult project, even though others believe that you can't, the thought that you will succeed will cause a member of the Elect to come forward in your mind. He is the one who brings the knowledge of all similar situations, both past and future, and this knowledge compared to your Heart of Man will cause a feeling of confidence to rise within you. The stronger your belief that you will succeed, the more he will come towards the front part of your mind.

There is a feeling caused by being conscious of the presence of God. You feel more wide-awake but it is the absence of all other feelings. Walking into an empty church will bring this feeling for some. This is a holy feeling. God is holy feelings.

The Holy Ghost, who is number two of the Elect, is fellowship. The right mental attitude towards a group of people with whom you have a mutual interest will cause this feeling.

The Spirit of Love is number three and is the feeling caused by wanting to make someone happy or to help him.

Number four on the Elect is the Spirit of Truth. The trinity of a soul is the Spirit of Love, the Spirit of Truth and the Holy Ghost. Where the Spirit of Truth is the Son of man, the Spirit of Love is the Daughter of women.

The lineup of the Elect is in the order of creation. Although all were created together, number two was finished in the long process of creation before number three, number three before number four, et cetera. It could be called an order of greatness, as it was necessary for each to be finished before the next one could be finished.

Some members of the Elect come forward in your mind, not because of thoughts you hold, but because of physical or bodily changes. One of these is called *Moloch* in the Bible. He is the feeling of pain. To be sacrificed on the altar of Moloch is to be tortured to death. Pain hurts because it is so intensely disliked. The one called Moloch has more than average unselfishness and higher than average ideals, and so when children were sacrificed to him, usually by fire, he disliked it intensely. That started the ball rolling in some of the preliminary plans of the universe, where the object was to get feelings started as a sensation, with no consciousness of knowledge. When you acquire certain knowledge through physical means that your Heart of Man dislikes, you feel it as pain. The more you dislike it and the further back in your ancestry the dislike goes, the stronger will you feel the pain.

How strong any feeling has to be in order to see the one who personifies it, will depend on how strong your inherited memories are of that same feeling. In olden times when people did not have so many ancestors, they did not have such strong inherited memories of feelings. It was easier for them to have feelings strong enough in relation to their inherited memory of it to see the particular member of the Elect who was bringing it to the front of their minds. If this member went too far and stepped in front of the person having the feeling, the feeling would disappear and that member would be stepping out into this world, and could be seen by other people. It was so easy to make Moloch step out that he became worshiped as a god, but his dislike of sacrifices was so great he tried to stop them himself.

Among the Elect there are kings, queens, princes, and princesses. The feelings caused by physical changes or bodily functions are called kings or queens, depending on their sex, which makes Moloch a king. The feelings which only males can normally experience have a prince behind each feeling. Feelings which only females can feel are caused by the princesses.

If everything else were equal, feelings would grow stronger with each generation; but everything that grows on this world, both plant and animal, has its growth controlled by the angels of the first heaven. Lucifer is the highest angel in the first heaven, and human feelings come through him. For his job he stands on the top of the first heaven. Lucifer is also number five on the Elect. He is next to Emmanuel, and the name of his position is the Intermediary. To have this position it is necessary to stand by God all day. If any mortal had to do this, he would shrivel up in the light. Someone who had no darkness in his own personality had to do this, and that was Lucifer. As an angel of the first heaven Lucifer had nothing to do until the human race finally reached this level.

The first one there was the same Adam mentioned in the Bible, for he was the first to have the members of the Elect in his mind. No one can go to heaven unless he was born across the top of the first heaven. All the ones before him went back to their ancestors when they died.*

The Story of Creation in Genesis, where the Bible speaks of man being created in a day, was translated from the Hebrew

---

*This information caused a feeling of surprise within me when I first remembered it, but I recall explaining this at an early age and then not thinking of it again—as if I had never known it.

into Greek and from the Greek into English. Biblical scholars have since found that in Hebrew the word used for day meant time, not one day.

From a religious point of view, the question of evolution should be simple enough. If the evolutionary theory is correct, that is the way God placed people on earth. If the theory of evolution is wrong, then God used some other way.

A speed-up in the evolutionary process is sometimes caused by freaks or mutations, but there are two general theories, the Lamarckian theory and the Darwinian.

The Lamarckian theory says that if fast-running animals such as deer can escape their enemies by nimbleness, then the fact that they try to run as fast as they can will gradually make them go faster. Giraffes continually trying to reach high leaves of trees will make their necks grow longer, and animals that try to hide from their enemies will gradually learn to hide better because of their continual trying.

The Darwinian theory of evolution says that if fast-running animals such as deer can escape their enemies by running away, then the fastest deer will get away more often than the slower ones. The fleetest deer thus produce speedier progeny. In the case of giraffes, the ones with the longest necks will have a better chance to survive in times of extreme drought, and the giraffe family will gradually develop longer necks. Animals that don't hide carefully enough from their enemies will be killed; those that do hide successfully will live to have offspring who inherit that same quality. It is a well-known fact among those who raise cattle that proper selection will build up the quality of the herd, and Darwin felt that selectivity by nature will accomplish the same end.

As for the Lamarckian theory of evolution, there has always been some argument whether acquired characteristics can be inherited. Whether they can or not depends on what the spirit of the animal thinks of it. When the tails were cut off from mice for fifty generations, the last generation were born with tails just as long as ever. The spirit was unconcerned. When an Italian bull pulled off its tail that was caught in a door, its offspring thereafter were born without tails. The spirit of the bull didn't like it.

Both of these evolutionary theories apply also to the human family. If a doctor could examine the parents of Adam or Eve, he would think they were normal. A mind reader would think differently. Physically the human race evolved slowly, but mentally it was more like a series of vertical steps. The biggest of these steps was at the time of Adam.

The first persons to go to heaven were some of Adam's descendants. Adam himself outlived many of them before he too went to heaven; those already there would plan another life for themselves in this world, then be born again. Everyone's life in those days was so planned that there could be no unhappiness in it. These were extremely happy times, but this happiness was borrowed from the future, allowing just enough time for Lucifer to make a devil out of himself.

Lucifer has one of the more important positions in the universe, but by the way he looks and seems physically and mentally, he is six years old. According to the scriptures, Lucifer is a cherub, defined as "a beautiful child" by the dictionary. A five-year-old girl, with a much better than average memory, told her mother that the devil was not the way people said he was, because she could remember him, and he was a young boy.

The human family was making such slow progress that Lucifer argued with those who went to heaven to try to get them to have more children. He succeeded, but it was a mistake for the people to listen to him. Lucifer claimed that he was a part of God, and that God was good, so he was good, also. Furthermore, he thought that he was superior to all those below him, including the rest of the first heaven.

Until that time, Lucifer had never done anything wrong. He didn't want to. If anyone else had thought what Lucifer thought, it would have done no harm. But human feelings grow through Lucifer. So, when Lucifer thought he was superior to some, those thoughts created a new feeling—pride.

Lucifer was wrong, because there is nothing better than good. Had he been good, he could not have made a mistake. He was not superior, because all souls are created and remain equal. It is just possessions and positions that are unequal. Lucifer had a position, and still does, that is superior to most, but *he* is not. Your intelligence and knowledge may be superior to some, but these are not a part of you any more than your money in the bank. Your personality is a possession; your soul is you.

Before there were any humans on Earth, Lucifer felt no particular feelings, had little to do but wait until the heathen or subhumans were born at his level. It was planned so that Lucifer and all angels would enjoy the same feelings that the people in the world felt.

At the time of the first humans in this world, which began with Adam, not many feelings could be enjoyed by the angels. Lucifer thought that if there were enough people so that all feelings would be felt at the same time, this would be better for all who received their feelings indirectly.

And in time, people began having children as fast as Lucifer wanted them to, and soon there were not enough people in heaven to help all those who had been born across the top of the first heaven and were still on the world. So many things went wrong with their lives that the average feelings of the world became more unhappy than happy. To keep from sharing their feelings, Lucifer severed his spiritual connection to the feelings of this world. From that time on no angel has experienced the feelings of this world, and all angels began to get tired of what they were doing.

In the first heaven the angels control the mechanics of everything that grows. The second heaven is for humans when they die. The angels of the third heaven regulate the material part of this universe. If a baseball is thrown in the air, it is supposed to come down, and it will, as long as these angels stay on the job.

If this world ran into another one, the two surfaces in contact would stop, but the weight behind the rest would keep moving, spattering like an egg thrown against a wall. The friction would generate intense heat. The only reason an egg breaks is that the front part of the egg stops when it hits, and the weight of the rest of it keeps on moving. If each particle of weight in this world could be stopped at the same time, no damage would occur. The whole world could even run backwards without hurting anything. From the third heaven this can be done by spiritual means.

The angels of the fourth, fifth, and sixth heavens control the first, second, and third, respectively. There could be three more heavens to control these three, continuing on forever. However, God is infinite and so the seventh heaven is controlled by Him.

Although everything in the universe can be seen from the seventh heaven, the only ones who live there are saints. Each member of the Elect was created for his particular work, but the saints were chosen.

It was desirable to create this universe by starting with eternity and planning it backwards, but it was necessary to start at the beginning. The first plans of this universe were so elemental that the people were not only as simple as bricks but they looked like bricks. Each one was no more than a position. Each time the universe was planned, it was run backwards to the beginning and planned over again. Each time more was added. So there was an infinite number of plans for a universe, but they were all preliminary to this one.

One reason was to build up feelings as strong as desired. For example, the first one to dislike pain was Moloch, but the next time the universe was planned, his ancestors didn't like that feeling, because he brought them his knowledge and dislike of it. Each time thereafter when it came Moloch's time to be born, he would inherit a stronger dislike of pain.

Feelings were thus not only made stronger, but each of the Elect had knowledge of the future situations that concerned him. If Adam was in danger and wished to escape, then the one who is fear would come to Adam's consciousness and bring the knowledge of all the future times when anyone was trying to escape something. This knowledge, plus the consciousness of the danger, would be compared to all of Adam's knowledge, both inherited and acquired; this act of comparison was itself the feeling of fear.

When one of Adam's sons had a feeling, nearly all of it

would be the same as it was for Adam. But not quite. A very small part of it would be an inherited memory of the emotion or feeling as it seemed to Adam, if it was a feeling that Adam had also felt.

Whenever you feel an ordinary feeling, about sixty percent of this is the inherited memory from your ancestors as it felt to them. The remainder is just knowledge compared to knowledge. On one side is the knowledge you acquired in this world, including every moment of your past added to what you inherited from your ancestors. On the other side is the knowledge of the situation you're in, added to all similar situations in the universe. The comparison of these two sides creates feeling.

To Adam, one hundred percent of his feeling was caused by knowledge compared to knowledge. Feelings have thus been getting stronger since Adam's time. But when a member of the Elect has the feeling that he is (such as the one who is fear feeling fear, the Spirit of Love feeling love), no one is coming up in his mind. Instead, all is an inherited memory, but stronger than that of anyone else.

The principle of creation is demonstrated here; it is the principle of something being created out of itself; the Elect causing their ancestors to have feelings, and in turn inheriting their own from their ancestors.

Out of all the people who were ever going to exist there were plenty of choices from which to pick saints, but each member of the Elect had to be built up, little by little, to fit perfectly at all times with the rest of the universe.

There is a sacrifice involved in becoming a saint. Many people are not going to live forever, and if any one of these had an opportunity to sacrifice his life for others and did, this would still not make him a saint, even though it would give him eternal life. However, there has been a choice given some of sacrificing their souls and going back to where they were before they were created, like thinning a row of vegetables to make it better for the ones that are left.

The ones who made this choice thought they were going to cease to exist; instead, they became saints. A saint-feeling is one in which it is all right with you to disappear completely, if God would have it that way. There needed to be one saint between each member of the Elect. For one thing, the saints help keep harmony in the rest of the universe.

There are some tough fellows among the Elect, and some who would have gone wandering off on their own against the rules, except that there can be no mutiny on this team. If any member of the Elect steps out of line, he steps on the track of a saint, which gives him a saintly feeling. This is one of the jobs of the saints, for no one gets unruly while he is feeling like a saint.

The first angel to get tired in the third heaven came down to this world and lived a normal but rather short human life. When he returned to heaven, he was as tired as he had been before. He asked God how it would be if he jumped off the top of the first heaven. God told him he would be completely unconscious. He could have come down and lived another life on this world. But he didn't like the life he had just lived, so he would rather become unconscious than go through that again. When he jumped, the people here could tell that something significant had come over the world. This was just before Adam died. Part of the spiritual connection Lucifer formerly had with this world he transferred to this angel. So the body of this unconscious angel became death.

At this time hell was created to balance things off. Meanwhile, Adam died, just in time to go to heaven before he would have been caught in death.

When people go to death, Lucifer inherits their memories and can remember their knowledge, just as if it were his own. One of Lucifer's possessions is the best memory next to God's. A memory of feelings is not the actual feelings themselves. To anyone who has never felt pain, the memory of it does not seem like much, and Lucifer himself has never felt pain.

All angels of the third heaven are milky white with an appearance similar to white smoke. When old people are nearing death, some of them begin to see it. It appears white and smoky, and they may actually believe the house is on fire. A few days before my father died, he became excited about so much smoke in the house. I told him that was not smoke but was pride and death.

Pride and death are the same place. The more anyone thinks he is superior, the deeper he enters this medium, which is the spirit of this world. The further he enters, the stronger he acquires the knowledge that he is good and superior. This is false knowledge but it is just as strong as if it were true. It is this total knowledge of being both good and superior that is compared to your Heart of Man that makes the feeling of pride.

At the beginning of pride on earth there were two pathways by which a person might enter, through Lucifer, into the feeling of pride. One was to believe you were good, the other to believe you were superior. If Lucifer no longer believes he is good, you can still feel very proud by believing you are superior. A chain of thoughts can force the belief that you are superior without your being aware of it. One way is to set up ideals and then attain them.

When anyone sets an ideal or goal, he makes it higher than he is himself. Once he attains this ideal or goal, he feels himself superior to what he used to be. But in the back of his head he knows that everyone is equal. This forces him to believe he is superior to everyone else, too.

It is easy to set up a goal while you are talking by merely thinking what kind of impression you want to make. When you attain this goal it causes the feeling of pride. Some people who do this, at the same time dislike the feeling of pride they experience. This makes a mental turmoil. They are apt to sound sensitive and self-conscious.

The way most people feel proud is to associate themselves with their possessions and positions. If these are superior to those of other people around them, they automatically think they are, too. When you feel proud about something, the object of your pride is usually all right; it is the feeling of pride that is wrong, for it is impossible to feel proud about anything without fooling yourself.

There are some feelings you have only when pride is mixed

with the situation. One of those is embarrassment. If you feel proud of your intellect and then say something ignorant or foolish, it will embarrass you. If you feel proud of your good manners and then commit a social faux pas, it can be embarrassing. But there are people who have never felt embarrassment in their life, and can't feel it, because they never feel pride. If they say something stupid, they may recognize that it is wrong, but they can't feel embarrassed. They are more likely to feel funny. Funny feelings are in a special class.

People may laugh to be polite, or as a relief for pent-up energy, of which there are many kinds with many causes; but when a person feels funny it is because of information that doesn't fit with the way his mind has been conditioned. Sometimes a situation will evoke a very funny feeling that is, at the same time, something sad. Sad and funny feelings at the same time can cause hysterics.

The world has felt proud for so long that each person has inherited memories of pride that rise to the surface whenever he thinks he is either good or superior. A mistake is to brag about someone. You may think you are honoring that person, but it is necessary to be good yourself in order to honor anyone. Therefore, it is impossible to think you are honoring someone without also thinking you are good. Thus, no one in this world can honor anyone else in this world. If any President of the United States ever visited you, this would be no honor, for it is his position that is superior. He is your equal, and nobody is good.

An easy way to feel proud is to agree with a person as he praises someone else. The words he is saying may be the truth, but if you agree with them completely you will also feel proud, because you will think you are good. You will think you are good, for you will think you are honoring someone, because you are agreeing with words that have that meaning.

One member of the Elect comes to your consciousness every time you feel proud and sad at the same time. When this choked-up feeling comes, you are usually feeling that you are honoring someone who is involved in a sad situation. While pride is involved in many small things, it is the spiritual reason for its existence that makes it so important.

After Lucifer created pride, he did things for the same reason boys have played malicious tricks on Halloween night. Also, if he could bring an end to human life on the world he knew he could then control the universe. Disease germs were created by angels from the first heaven who thought Lucifer would win if they helped him. If this makes Lucifer seem too naive, it should be remembered that his age remains the same as when he started, as it does for all angels.

All wars, disease, crime, and accidents can be blamed on Lucifer. But all these had to happen in order to make good things seem good. One of the big troublemakers on this world has been pride. When people feel proud, they very seldom realize its cause. They may even believe they did not feel proud when they did. When you feel proud, you do not talk to yourself and say that you are good or superior. These beliefs may be the result of a chain of subconscious thoughts. You may determine the truth of these statements the next time you feel proud, by analyzing your own thoughts.

To help to prove the truth about feelings a likely place to look is in what you feel in relation to anything requiring skill. In such activities there are usually one or more special feelings that will help you to be successful, if you are obedient to those feelings.

I could feel the spirit behind baseball easier than any other. With less than two out, a runner on third, the batter hits a grounder to the third baseman. Should the runner go back to third and allow the batter to be put out at first, or would it be better for his team if he allows himself to be chased back and forth while the batter goes on to second base? The right way depends on the running ability of the runner and the playing skill of the other team. I could make the right play by feeling strongly enough the spirit behind baseball, and let the feeling tell me.

When a new boy moved to my town, whom I had never seen or heard of before, I could tell without seeing him play just how well he could play ball. To do this, I had to remember strongly the feeling of playing ball and let it tell me about him. This is possible, for our feelings have the same spirits as for everyone else. It is this way for many things, such as boxing, playing musical instruments, et cetera. This feeling becomes stronger and tells you more definitely how much ability the other person has, if he talks about it.

Your feelings can do this, because a substantial part of each feeling is caused by a member of the Elect who comes into your consciousness. This makes you conscious of his knowledge, if he comes in far enough, and he already knows all about the other person on this particular subject. Disconcertingly so, for if there is a group of one hundred girls in which just one girl is not as good as the rest, some fellows will have feelings that will enable them to pick her out as though she were painted red, and for the purpose of getting her into deeper trouble than she is in already. If she makes a definite effort and changes her ways, the same feelings will no longer make those fellows want to talk to her.

While most sexual feelings are personified by members of the Elect, there are also other spirits involved. The foundation of this world, however, rests on the work of the Elect.

4

Work of the Elect

In addition to the Elect being most of the feelings, each is the spirit behind an animal family, a bird family, a fish family, and a plant family. The involuntary organs of fish, birds, and animals work the way they are supposed to because they work that way in the spirit behind them. Each of the Elect is the spirit behind something to eat in the vegetable kingdom, as well as a flower and usually hundreds of other herbs and trees, all of the same family.

Some people like flowers better than others do, because of knowledge they acquired about flowers before they were born. They can't recall the knowledge, but because of it they experience strong feelings while looking at flowers. A flower expresses the love life of the one who is the spirit behind it.

The traits that each member of the Elect inherited would resemble a tree, if a drawing of them were made. If any man went back through his hereditary characteristics as far as possible, he would have to start with what he inherited from his father, then his father's father, and so on in the male line. A woman would have to start with her mother, then her mother's mother, and stay on the female line. In this way one could go all the way back to his first ancestor, God.

If anyone went off on any other line of ancestry, it would be like going off on the branches of a tree instead of up the main trunk. A tree looks the way it does because the spirit behind it has a hereditary tree of the same general appearance. But certain characteristics, mostly female, are used in making a fruit tree.

But there is something more important than these four families of which each member of the Elect is in control. They are the parts of your body. In each part a different member of the Elect has control. The parts are where your feelings originate.

The Holy Ghost has the heart, all except the valves— the one who is fear lives there. The Spirit of Love is the nerves, the Spirit of Truth is the blood. Blood is manufactured in the hollow part of your bones where it is better protected. Here Emmanuel lives. Whenever you aim at the truth well enough to feel it, you literally feel it in your bones.

Whenever you have certain feelings, it is possible to tell where they originate. The one who makes weird feelings is the spirit behind hair. These feelings are felt with the roots of your hair. Strong enough weird feelings will make your hair move slightly.

Because most of the feeling is now an inherited memory, it is usually impossible to tell where the feeling originates. It is possible, for example, to like tools so well that it makes for a definite feeling independent of happiness or pride caused by getting new tools. This one is the spirit behind fingernails and toenails. Something to work with, such as a scraper or pincers, is a tool. Everyone has tools on the end of his fingers.

There are different kinds of bossy feelings, but there is a feeling when you remain conscious of your competence; and when you possess a competent and confident executive feeling, you feel it with your brains. This same member of the Elect is the spirit behind the pineapple in the plant kingdom, and he is the Spirit behind all dogs in the animal world.

Because the spirit behind dogs is also the spirit behind human brains, dogs have the ability to pick up mental qualities from individual people, if they are acquainted and like the people well enough. An exceptionally friendly dog is merely a dog that adopts that type of personality from a person of the same type. If a person has mental characteristics he does not want anyone else to know, he should not own a dog.

Large dogs can pick up human characteristics very easily. A jealous person could own a dog so jealous that it is dangerous. Some people become so agitated over the wrongdoings of others that their dogs may bite when they think a person is doing wrong.

The acquired traits that a dog picks up from human beings

should not be confused with instincts. A dog that is tied up may bite, because his ancestors were used for guard duty. Now the dog has strong instincts to guard whatever he is tied to.

A chow dog may become wild if he is fed meat, because his ancestors ate meat, until they were tamed by the Chinese. The Chinese could not afford meat for their dogs, so they were fed some other food. When fed meat, it recalls an instinct with a deep root from wild ancestors. Where human instincts cause evil, it is the love of money that has the deepest root.

All animals think like a person who makes up his mind so strongly that he can't change it, so it is very important to get animals started on the right track the first time and never allow them to acquire bad habits. Dogs, however, are the only animals that pick up personality traits naturally from human beings, which they do because of the unique position of the spirit behind the dog family.

The place one would most expect to find competent and confident executive feelings would be in the brain. Likewise, down through the ages fear has been spoken of as existing in the heart. Weird feelings are supposed to stand your hair on end, and the rest of the Elect and their work would fit in an appropriate way, if all the facts were known.

Each gland in our bodies has one of the Elect behind it, and the function of each gland corresponds with the job of that particular member of the Elect. There is one of the Elect for each eye and ear; these four are kings. There is also a queen whose job it is to convert certain physical stimuli into feelings. She controls the skin, both internal and external skin. Every position on the Elect has a name, and one is named Doctor. He must recognize any feeling caused by an injury or disorder to any part of your body. Otherwise, you might feel pleasure when you should feel pain.

Those Elect who are not kings or queens are they whose feeling is caused entirely by a thought, whether of escape from danger, the anticipation of something good, the thought that you must be careful in what you are doing, or any of the rest.

It is the thought that causes that member of the Elect to come forward in your mind, bringing with him all the knowledge of that same situation that has ever happened or will happen during the rest of this age. A thought is the discovery of a fact, or at least the belief that you have discovered a fact.

Some thoughts arise so fast and automatically that it is difficult to see they came before the feeling. But they do, except for the kings and queens or where drugs or stimulants are used.

Lucifer is the spirit behind poppies from which opium is made, and the use of opium will cause a feeling of pride in a person whether he wants it or not. If a man had always felt proud of his toughness and his ability to win in a fight against anyone his size, he would have a tendency to become violent upon taking opium. But if he was the kind of person who kept out of fights and felt proud of his intellectual accomplishments and appreciated beautiful things, he would then think opium had a wonderful effect—but only when he began taking it. The use of any drug or stimulant to create feelings will always have a reaction each time, and the reaction, though usually slight, is always opposite to the main feeling of euphoria, and fairly permanent. Therefore, the effect accumulates with each use, and the victim continually needs a larger dose to produce the same effect.

The feeling caused by drugs is created by the same principle of knowledge compared to knowledge. Only, instead of a member of the Elect bringing the knowledge up to the front part of your mind because of what you think, it comes through the use of a drug of which he is the spirit. If the drug is opium it would be Lucifer, and that would give you the feeling he is responsible for, which is pride. Alcohol and drugs produce this effect and, in excess, cause complete degeneration of the spirit. The first time one takes drugs or strong drink is the critical time, because of the reaction involved.

Each member of the Elect was given particular rules to follow. There is one who comes up close in your consciousness, and you can feel her knowledge every time she sees you are sick.

The sicker you are, the further up she comes. This knowledge of all the sickness in the human family, when compared to your Heart of Man, can cause a very sick feeling.

God is the egg and male sperm cell. Emmanuel's mother, who is also on the Elect, is a mother feeling. She is involved with unborn babies and their mothers. There is a religious ceremony in which she is called the mother of God. This is ambiguous, for since God owns all mothers, everyone who is a mother is God's mother. Still, she is more a mother just as Emmanuel is more a son.

A genuine miracle would not seem impressive if it were understood or if it were commonplace. There is no miracle mentioned in the Bible any greater than why a tree grows.

When the male sperm cell and egg unite, something makes the combination start to grow. And whatever it is that does this, if it wanted to it could make the egg grow by itself. Of course, it would not be an ordinary baby, and when it grew into a man it would not be an ordinary man. But that is what happened in Emmanuel's case.

Each part of your body has some life independent of the rest, because the one who is behind it has life. Nevertheless, your life is in the blood, as the life of a tree is in the sap.

The character of each member of the Elect is reflected in the work he does. Some members of the Elect have what might be called a hard character. They cannot be pushed around by other people and might even enjoy a fight. These Elect are the spirits behind hard-shell nuts. Someone of an opposite character will produce something of an opposite nature. For example, Emmanuel's mother, who is the opposite from a hard character, is the spirit behind pear trees.

It is easy to notice the similarity in appearance between any part of the human body and something that is good to eat in the plant kingdom. For instance, a bean is shaped like a kidney. The pituitary gland is like a peanut. Some have the same shape as a bunch of grapes, and so on. The Elect who is the spirit behind a particular plant family deliberately tried to make the main part of the plant to be eaten resemble that part of the body of which he is also the spirit. A pineapple is supposed to resemble a brain, but some members of the Elect, such as the Spirit of Love, have parts of the body that are practically shapeless, such as the nerves. So, she used the mammary glands as a model for the fruit of the lemon tree.

A member of the Elect who is the spirit behind some part of the body of one sex, but not of the opposite sex, will also be either a prince or princess and have the type of feeling that is felt by that one sex. For example, Emmanuel's mother, who is the spirit behind the uterus, is also a mother feeling, something men cannot feel.

Something else that was very unusual about Emmanuel's mother was that she was the first one who ever grew old enough to become a mother, before the spirit of this world, which is pride, separated her from an immaculate condition that nearly all have when they are born. She was not yet in the spirit of this world.

Some young children today can *see* pride, because they are not yet in it. For them to do so, there must be other people close by who are feeling strong pride. If babies see its white and smoky character, they will start to cry. I can remember being made aware of this manifestation more than once. It looked as if the atmosphere was becoming visible around the one who was full of pride.

All those who can see pride will have a very delicate expression about their eyes, especially at the sides and without a trace of sunken look. But when a number of people who are big enough spiritually are standing close enough while feeling pride, those who can see pride will not be able to stand it. Their eyes will take on a sunken look. And if the spirit of this world penetrates far enough, that look will be permanent. George Washington is a classic example. He must have been several years old and tried hard to keep his eyes from changing, while others around him were feeling very proud.

Many have made their eyes change on purpose. It seemed to them like getting hold of something and pulling it into themselves. If one who can see pride pulls it into himself while he is thinking why he wants to do this, it will give him a very thoughtful look, which will remain with him the rest of his life.

Before the expression of anyone's eyes changes, there are possible feelings in his body such as pride, anger, and even slight sexual feelings that cannot be felt without great harm, causing the expression to change at that time. Each feeling will cause a different kind of look. Erogenous feelings, such as back-scratching, should not be experienced. These feelings are not strong enough to force a person into the spirit of this world, but will cause a condition that makes his two front teeth lap over.

The reason for this is that when you pull in pride, you are also pulling in a new set of instincts. Before that time your instincts began with your first ancestors and came up to the time of Adam, but no further. The condition stays this way until the arrival of the spirit of this world, which is when the expression of your eyes change. From then on, your inherited memories reach out and include all the knowledge of your parents to within a year before your birth.

Those who have experienced this condition after becoming old enough to talk about it, have always referred to the two states as their old self and their new self. Their old self is their Heart of Man, where the most recent instinct is from the time of Adam. The new Heart of Man goes back from the present generation through Adam, so that Adam and Eve form a connecting link between the old and new Heart of Man.

While you are still in your old self, before your eyes change, if you experience feelings that can only be felt by your new self, the feelings will force the changeover at that time. Erogenous feelings will pull on the two sets of instincts at the same time, causing tension.

When one who can see pride is made to believe that he is good or superior, it will force his eyes to change. The upper eyelid will come up too far, causing a stare because of the effort to keep pride out, although its cause is internal. It seems to the victim like a contest with the devil, and in a sense it is.

Anyone who gets angry at the devil before he is born will be born with red hair, even if none of his ancestors ever had red hair. Some redheads tell the devil what they think of him before they are born, but after they leave the top of the first heaven. They stand with their weight on one leg and twist around to look back. This results in legs of unequal length and a deformed back. The time this takes will seem like a matter of seconds to those doing it, but nine months will go by on this world, as these occur on different time planes.

Some argue with the devil that they are too small to help him. If they argue very long or strong, they will be midgets. Many of those who got angry at the devil figure out how to get their hair back to its natural color by pulling in their new self while they think why they are doing it. This kind will have a very thoughtful expression to their eyes. If they do nothing about it, their hair will stay red all of their lives if they were angry enough. In that case, their hair color can be inherited by their children. However, red hair would die out in three generations if no one ever again got mad at the devil before birth.

Some babies pull their new selves in so they can cry louder. This makes a fine line near the outside edges of their eyes. Many make this change-over so they can like the world better. This will cause a bulge above their upper eyelids going out towards the sides. If a person pulls in his new self so he can feel the Spirit of Love feeling stronger, it will make his eyes look smaller.

If the love feeling is for a person, it will make only the small look about the eyes. If the love is for an animal, it will also cause the nose to grow long. If the love is for an inanimate object, such as a doll or a teddy bear, in addition to the small eyes and long nose there will be a wide and bulbous look to the nose. A classic example here would be Jimmy Durante.

The babies who can see pride if others around them are feeling proud will dislike this sensation very intensely. For that reason, babies should not be taken to a theater or other places where many people might feel proud. When babies see the pride that others feel, they see what a spiritualist would call ectoplasm, or death.

If a baby feels some pain, as from a diaper pin sticking him, the baby can escape most of the feelings by backing away from a wide-awake state of consciousness and go so far back within his instincts that his feelings will be dulled and he can better stand the pain. But he will not be able to come all the way back to the instincts from his recent ancestors, and he will remain retarded all of his life.

If an injury is a part of it, such as a spinal injury caused by lifting the baby without putting a hand under the head, he may go all the way back through his instincts and apparently die in his sleep from unknown causes. Babies receive some of their permanent looks by what they think at the time they pull their new selves in between their old selves and their present state of consciousness. Also, important personality traits may be formed then.

Looks of good-intention are caused by people who think they are not completely born until they are born into the spirit of this world, too. So, they pull their new selves in almost as soon as they are born.

When a baby loses his old set of instincts, those instincts ascend. If he can pull them back after that, he will lift himself to a position in the first heaven. While he is there he can see that some people are the color of red-hot iron; some are like iron that is starting to get cold; and some will be extra bright. This brightness represents unselfishness acquired by wanting to help others before they began planning their own lives. At that time also each person's smartness was determined by how hard he tried to get what he wanted, either for others or himself. Few can remember if they did pull back their old selves. I can remember doing so.

Emmanuel was twelve years old when the expression of his eyes changed because of the spirit of this world. Before the expression of your eyes changes, it is impossible to do anything morally wrong. Afterwards, it is impossible not to, except with the right spiritual help. In Emmanuel's case when the expression of his eyes changed, he was still able to keep from being influenced by the spirit of this world. And his virgin birth helped prevent waywardness caused by instincts.

God's spirit, called the Holy Spirit, was withheld until he

was baptized. After that, since the spirit of this world could not interfere, he could then see everything that he wished to know about for the rest of his life, until he was crucified. So, his Heart of Man remained constant all his life. Before he was twelve he was much the same as others before the expression of their eyes changes.

Everyone's body is a temple, but a veil prevents you from seeing how the ones work who live there. Until the expression of your eyes changes, so that you are not yet living in the spirit of this world, you are really living in the temple. Emmanuel's mother lived that way longer than any woman before her.

I have known several who have gone through this experience of change, after they became old enough to talk. In each case it seemed to them they are entirely different persons and that their old selves are better than their new. In my case, I remember thinking a few days later that I liked listening to music better than I had before.

This change will become very difficult to remember later in life, even for those who reach an age of five to ten years before they lose their old self. The reason is that feelings and instincts that come from your old self have no immoral content. At the time you feel them, they seem much better, but later you remember them as weaker and more dream-like.

The most interesting thing about anyone who can still see pride—whose inherited memories only come up to the time Lucifer made a devil out of himself—is the fact that he can talk to God in plain words, like talking over a telephone. He asks a question, then listens.

When talking to boys, God uses their mothers' voices, and when talking to girls, their fathers' voices. There have been many children who talked to God and thought they were talking to one of their parents, when that parent was not there. Many more of those who could have talked to God never knew they could and so never tried.

God never volunteers any information, because the plans for the universe are already as perfected as possible. Had they not been, they would have been changed in the beginning. Those who are near enough to talk with God are almost back to where they were before they were created. In the beginning there was just God, and all that holds them out now as individuals is their ignorance. If they could have God's knowledge without asking for it, they would disappear in a flash without leaving a trace.

There are babies who talk to God who have not yet learned to talk in this world. Anyone can talk when he is a baby, or before he is born, by using the second stage of aiming at the truth.

There are three stages of aiming at the truth. In the first, the Spirit of Truth looks at all of your past memories on this world to pick out the right words or ideas, according to what you want. This is the power you use every day in your speech and thoughts. In this stage the Spirit of Truth only looks back to when you were born. The closer your association with the Spirit of Truth, the greater choice of words or ideas he gives you.

If you could use the second stage, you would be using your smartness for a memory. In this stage the Spirit of Truth looks at all your knowledge, all the way back before you were born. Using this stage, you can remember the plans of your life including the future.

If you could use the third stage, you would be aiming at the truth the way God does, and could explain anything, even in a foreign language that you didn't understand yourself.

The third stage is very rare, but the second is more common than might be supposed. The younger you are, the more available it is. You could know a lot more about the spiritual side of this universe when you were a baby than you will ever know again in this life.

Not many can still use the second stage, once they are old enough to talk. Even if they can, all they can usually remember is the easiest parts, such as how to read.

When a baby is remembering the plans of its life, a day-dreamy look, like a sheen or film, will come over its eyes. This will go away as soon as it quits remembering the plans of the future.

If a child three years old could read well without learning, he would still have to learn to read later on. By the time he grew up, it would have to be something as important as meeting someone he was going to marry later on, before he could use the second stage. All it might do then is to make that person seem very familiar.

When you are sound asleep, you may easily know the future, for there are two types of spiritual dreams and two of worldly dreams. These last help prevent you from waking up. One of these is an imaginary reason for a sensation over which you have no control. If you hear someone hammering while you are asleep, you may dream that you are watching carpenters building a house. Or, if you are feeling sick, you might dream you are eating something disagreeable that is causing the upset feeling. The awakening stimulus being physical in this first type.

The second worldly dream of this type is caused by remembering the feelings or main impressions received during the recent past. Instead of the memory recalling you to wakefulness, you merely dream something that explains the incident well enough and go on sleeping. This is the common type of dream. If the dream contains problems, you may also dream answers to those problems. While what causes dreams is usually from the recent past, dreams can also result from unpleasant decisions you made with intensity when very young, producing recurring dreams of the same nature. This type of dream is interpreted in psychoanalysis.

Of the two types of spiritual dreams, one is merely parts of your future during this lifetime. Your smartness is used as a memory to produce this dream. The other is anything of a spiritual nature that you knew before you were born. This may include some things from a future lifetime, and is usually dreamed in color.

It is possible to have strong feelings while asleep, though it is more important to understand the feelings you have while awake. The most important feelings are the ones that are used to make eternity more enjoyable, called profit feelings.

5

Profit Feelings

Our present Heart of Man contains so much trouble that, by comparison, many things in this world will produce pleasure and happiness. However, we are not living in the age of happy times but in the age of work, where the object of the work is to make eternity better.

When this world was planned, it was desirable to make feelings become very strong, and many ways were used to accomplish this. Yet, no matter how strong a feeling is, if it is neither enjoyable nor miserable, it is not worth much.

Some feelings would be neutral if nothing were done about them—they would seem neither good nor bad. One of these is excitement. Your house burning down will cause high excitement, but there is nothing good about it. So two members of the Elect are used to make excitement enjoyable.

Whenever you think in a way which produces excitement, one of the Elect comes forward in your mind, bringing the knowledge of every situation that ever happened that caused that kind of thinking. This knowledge, compared to your Heart of Man, makes about forty percent of your feeling of excitement; it also pulls up the memory of each time your ancestors felt excitement. Your oldest instincts are the lowest; your latest instincts the highest; and your own memories are on top of this. Your consciousness is the apex.

The Elect who is excitement is not concerned with whether you enjoy it or not, but when you feel excitement that you like, another member of the Elect comes to the fore. He makes you have the knowledge of each time anyone liked excitement.

This shows how some feelings can be made to seem either good or bad, for excitement could have been made bad instead of good by not having a member of the Elect to like excitement, and by having one to dislike excitement every time it was connected with something bad. But this was not done, and excitement is being made into something good for eternity.

Feelings such as sadness, embarrassment, loneliness, odd or stupid feelings, self-consciousness and many more, people dislike to feel. But these feelings had to be built up until they became strong, so that opposite feelings will be liked stronger.

Behind each of the feelings that people dislike is a member of the Elect who brings the knowledge of that kind of situation up to the conscious part of our minds where we can feel it. There will come a time, however, when these feelings will be replaced. Each member of the Elect who now has a job of bringing up the knowledge of situations that are disliked will be given a new job.

For example, the one who now makes self-conscious feelings will be the one to appreciate mechanical design. When anyone appreciates certain kinds of mechanical design it causes a weak feeling, because the feeling is caused by what he alone thinks at the moment, compared to all the rest of his knowledge. Yet this can be a very good feeling.

The enjoyable feelings for eternity include all of those that do not interfere with other enjoyable feelings, to the extent that they do more harm than good. That was the only rule used in determining what feelings would be used for eternity.

If it were not for the fact that getting drunk interfered with wide-awake happiness and other feelings (besides interfering with the workings of the Elect in anyone's body) drunkenness could have been included. Lewd and licentious feelings interfere with all marital feelings, but especially in connecting the physical or sexual side of marriage with the platonic or Spirit of Love feelings of marriage.

If feelings are *not* relative, this treatise is fundamentally wrong. But most people should be able to discover evidence in their own lives to prove it. The truth of the theories that feelings are knowledge compared to knowledge and that this world is planned are both indicated by the feelings that some women have.

For example, of three different women one was contented and happy with the sexual side of her marriage. The second was more successful than average with her marriage, but in planning her life she had to try hard to keep things on an even keel, and in so doing endured many anxious moments. The third stormed her way through two marriages with attendant disorder and confusion.

The first received periodic feelings of strong contentment, which she enjoyed. The second felt anxiety every month, and the third described the way she felt as a mess. Besides misery and discomfort resulting from some physical disorder, which may be caused by something as simple as the wrong diet, all normal women have knowledge of the sexual side of their lives from beginning to end each time.

In *A Research in Marriage* by Dr. G. V. Hamilton (Medical Research Press, New York, Copyright 1929) it was claimed that after a hundred married women were carefully questioned, their answers indicated a definite relationship between an unhappy sex life and a tendency to have marked pre-menstrual depressions. Freedom from such a tendency is likely to be associated with a relatively adequate marital relationship. No reason was given for this condition, which was believed to be psychological rather than physiological.

Both the feeling and the cause are shown in the case where I heard a girl decribe her feelings by saying, "I start out sitting on top of the world, and then I hit the bottom of the ocean." She was married in her early twenties and liked her husband even better after their marriage than before. It was a blissful state for a matter of months, until his personal mistakes caught up with him, and he left her permanently.

If a woman puts little importance on the sexual side of her life, this knowledge compared to her Heart of Man will cause no feeling. Two girls who have the same experiences may have different feelings because of ancestors who were completely different in their reactions to sex.

Besides special exceptions there can be many kinds of disorders as indicated by one statistical examination of four thousand women which revealed fifty-two percent as having some degree of pain and difficulty.

Even though the job of making eternity perfect will be done, there are some ways that are much easier than others of doing the same thing. The easiest way is to do it the right way. The right way is referred to in Matt. 11:29, "Take my yoke upon you, and learn from me; for I am gentle and lowly in heart, and you will find rest for your souls."

When you are yoked to someone else, you are both doing the same work. If you are yoked to the Spirit of Truth, you are then helping to build the Lord's house, which will be used for eternity. There will then be no more misery of any kind.

The time when there will be no more feelings that people dislike will be after the second coming of Christ. The Heart of Man, from the time Lucifer made a devil out of himself until the second coming of Christ, has so much misery in it that everything good that happened to the human race feels good by comparison. The Lord's house, which is made of profit feelings and is all misery, will take the place of the present Heart of Man.

A large amount of misery that you tried to avoid when you planned your life is not worth as much as a small amount of misery that can be used for profit, in the work of making eternity better. A *profit feeling* is a feeling that you not only dislike, such as pain and misery, but which you planned out on purpose, before you were born, to make yourself feel in this life.

When people plan their lives to have a good time yet make so many mistakes that they become miserable, there is no profit in these feelings. Even though miserable feelings make other feelings seem better by comparison, the world would never get any place trying to have a good time during this age.

The Lord's house is made out of every kind of disagreeable feeling that exists. Every good feeling has its counterpart which will be included. And all profit feelings were planned out on purpose by those who feel them.

Whenever you enjoy any feeling, you would enjoy it even more if your ancestors had been more miserable. No matter in which direction your enjoyment lies, such as a feast or in playing games, if your ancestors had felt more misery in the opposite direction—that is, in being hungry or being left out of social gatherings—this would make the comparison stronger and the enjoyment greater. So, the Lord's house which is being built now to take the place of the Heart of Man is all misery.

There has to be one house built for each 664 people, and it is these same people who make all the profit feelings for their particular house. The whole world is divided into teams where God is number one, and number 666 is a special position with no feelings. If the Elect could make enough misery for the whole world, the rest of the world would not need the trouble it always has had. But the Elect can only make miserable feelings for itself; there must be one Lord's house for each team. The last house built is for the Elect themselves. So, the last shall be first, the first last.

There are many profit feelings, but the amount of time each one has to be felt for each house is three days. It doesn't matter whether just one person makes all of a particular profit feeling for his house, or whether it is divided with each one helping, as long as it adds up to three days of feeling at its maximum degree.

If you were helping to create a profit feeling by feeling some misery at a low degree, you would have to feel it for such a long time that you would just as soon feel it at a higher degree for a shorter time.

Things repeat themselves in cycles. Every day has four divisions, with a different feeling connected with each: a morning feeling; another from noon until evening; one until midnight; and the last from midnight until morning. Similarly, a different feeling is connected with each of the four seasons. There are also times of youth, adulthood, middle age, and old age. If it were not for the four seasons and ages, living would become monotonous before the end of a normal lifetime. There need to be periods of the day, seasons of the year, and times of your life.

In the age when the Lord's house is just beginning to be used, the old Heart of Man will have been removed. There will be no inherited knowledge or inherited feelings that have anything immoral connected with them. Feelings will be stronger and better than they are today, because the Lord's house is made of strong misery. Also, there will be many more kinds of desirable feelings that are almost nonexistent today. These will be made by the members of the Elect who now have feelings that no one likes.

When the Lord's house begins to be used, all feelings during the first generation will be simply knowledge compared to knowledge. But when the next generation has a feeling, a very small part will be inherited from what it seemed like to their parents. This will cause feelings to gradually get stronger, and in a few thousand years, all feelings will again be made mostly of an inherited nature. But all inherited memories of that time will be coming from a new Heart of Man. And this new Heart of Man can go on forever, for there will be no evil in it.

All people will go through their lives on this world and back to the second heaven, where there will be interesting things to do helping this world for a while; then into God, where each will plan for himself another life on this world. Each time they are born everything will seem as new as it did the first time. People will be born over and over again, and will be the ones who are saved out of the present time from Adam to the second coming of Christ.

There need be no special reward awaiting in heaven for those who try hard to live right during this lifetime. That is like climbing a mile-high ladder, where the reward is discovered to be a lot of muscle; the reward automatically goes with the job. Trying hard to live right makes good feeling more enjoyable.

The world will gradually pass through all ages, so that at one time you will live in the age where man is just learning to build a fire. This could be as exciting and pleasant as any other age.

Scientific research can be as interesting and enjoyable as any game. When one doesn't like it, it is usually because of his early environment. In the future, everyone will have his mind untangled, and so people will be interested in everything. In the age of happy times, the world is not going to stand still at a constant level of knowledge; knowledge will be continually increased. There is an answer, although it is not a yes or no answer, to the question of whether it is possible or not to learn all knowledge.

The thousands of miscellaneous scientific experiments made each year are like starting with the leaves of a tree, or the points on the needles of a fir tree, and working in that way to the center. But it is also possible to know the fundamental knowledge of the universe that supports the rest, like the trunk of a tree, and to know all principles; starting thus, you can arrive at the answer to any problem.

When the world reaches the age where science has discovered all fundamental knowledge, the whole cycle can be run through again. Every time the world is started over again, the plans of the world, including the evolutionary progress of the human family, can be run over at high speed until people have at least learned to talk before they start being born again.

In the history of this present world every kind of witchcraft and evil spirit has existed. None of this will be necessary in the new world of the future. In it, scientific research will eventually discover everything of a spiritual nature, but this will be among the last of the things to be discovered. It is necessary to understand the spiritual side of creation before it is possible to understand the material side, for the material side is not what it appears to be.

An important reason for the existence of all the evil spirits that were manifest on this world until a few centuries ago, was to force the average man of that time into a religious frame of mind. Without any more belief in the supernatural there will come a falling away from religion.

Similarly, after pride has been completely eliminated for a few hundred years, there will be history students who will argue that there were never any wars. They will argue that a few individuals might have fought a few other individuals, but that a whole nation of people could not all want to kill the people of any other nation. Trying to understand wars then will be as hard as trying to understand the supernatural now.

In the future world there will be no need for anything so evil that it will force man to go in the opposite direction. However, when the people of that day try to discover the ultimate reality of the physical world, they will also have to understand the spiritual world, for the material side of reality and the mental are inextricably linked together.

6

Poltergeist

The material side of this world with which we are all familiar, appears to be real enough, but it is not as solid as it seems. There have been many well-documented cases of supernatural phenomena showing that certain types of reality can be very insubstantial. When it cannot be reproduced at will, it cannot be studied by science.

The way the mental or spiritual side of this universe predominates over the physical or material side can be seen through some unusual happenings. The German word for the movement of objects by some non-physical force is *poltergeist, polter* meaning noise and *geist* meaning ghost. It is possible to deliberately create this phenomenon.

In this age of experimentation, it might seem foolish to tell everyone of an interesting experiment, then tell them not to try it. Yet a wise rule has always been never to experiment with things of a spiritual nature. Creating a poltergeist may be too difficult for the average researcher, anyway, and that is just as well.

The distance between things of the spirit and things of the world can be very close. While hypnotism may not be spiritual, and while mesmerism always is, the steps between them may overlap. They arrive at the same destination by different routes. When a person makes up his mind so firmly that it stays that way, this form of self-hypnotism is used in the making of a poltergeist.

Making objects move without any physical reason could be done by being born with a direct connection to God; so that when you think for something to move, it does. And there is a way to make such a temporary connection in an uncontrolled way; when that happens, it is called a poltergeist, a form of force.

To make a poltergeist you would have to find someone who can make up his mind and have him make it up on three separate subjects. The average person today may be a shade smarter than the average person of a few hundred years ago. This might help in making up one's mind, but worldly feelings are so great today that you may never come in contact with an adult who can totally make up his mind.

When a number of people have the same kind of feeling at the same time, it creates a strong spirit that can be felt by others who may not even be doing the same thing. If it is strong enough, it might be called a craze, such as we had for miniature golf and other games during the years of the depression. This can be strong enough to make someone want to do it who might not have thought much about it otherwise. All worldly feelings have to be pushed aside for you to make up your mind, and we are rarely used to any such all-out effort.

The origin of all feelings is knowledge compared to knowledge. But the sensation which this causes can not only be picked up through a long line of ancestors; you can also pick up this sensation of feelings from the rest of the world, in a small degree. People are not as individualistic as they appear. An enthusiastic audience creates a strong spirit.

There is a member of the Elect behind the feeling of panic. In a crowded building that catches on fire, the feeling of panic you would pick up from the crowd becomes so great that you would have to be a strong character to keep from thinking the thought that would cause that member to come rushing to the front of your mind. The thought is, "I must save myself at all cost."

The degree of feelings you pick up this way will depend upon how many people are involved, how close to them physically you are, how strong they are feeling their emotion which you are picking up from them, and how well you enjoy this feeling.

The spirit behind communism is created by many people

pooling their desires and abilities for gain. When thus owned by the people in common, it is called communism. Whether it is in a labor union or the Russian government makes no fundamental difference. In the book of Revelation, this spirit is called a beast.

A few hundred years ago, there were so few worldy feelings that people could think something strong enough to influence themselves for the rest of their lives. There was a time before that when they could think something strongly enough to influence others. If this was for evil, it was called a curse. There is such strong interference from worldly feelings today, a person who could make up his mind so completely would probably be quite young.

A poltergeist can come about accidentally when someone is thinking about one subject and realizes that, to understand the subject completely, he has to see its relationship to another subject. So, he makes up his mind that every time he thinks of the first subject, he will also think of the second subject. He will later be thinking of the second subject when he will notice its relationship to a third subject. So, he makes up his mind to always think of this third subject whenever he thinks of the second. After this, he will be thinking of the third subject when he notices its relationship to the first one. If he now makes up his mind to always think of the first one every time he thinks of the third one, he will have three subjects that are connected together. Any time during the rest of his life when he thinks of any one of these, he will think of the next one; but he will not be able to stop, for his mind is made up. No one can change his mind if it is really made up.

If his mind is made up to think of how one subject is connected to the next, instead of just remembering each one, then the first time around would be slow enough so that he could be talking about it and explaining the connection. He would not be able to stop this spiral of "circular" thinking. He would be able to recognize each of the three subjects after they appear too fast to talk about. Soon they will become too fast even to recognize. This buzzsaw effect will seem to be going away as it increases in speed. In less than a minute after the three subjects get a good start, they will reach the speed of infinity—another name for God.

Most people who have been able to do this have had their minds made up to just remember, rather than explain each one. And they made up their minds when they were so young that when they do think of one, it will start off on a circle so vague and fast that they never realize what has happened. In a few seconds it will reach the speed of infinity, and immediately after that if anyone close by concentrates hard on some object, it will move, especially if someone starts to pick it up, which makes him think about it. It is apt to move sideways. If it is a stack of dishes that crash to the floor, they will be noisy. Reports on these cases claim an extra-loud noise is produced when an object moved by this force hits something solid. So, this phenomenon became known as a noisy ghost, although it has nothing to do with either a ghost or any haunted house.

It does show that the reality of this world has an explanation that rests on a mental or spiritual foundation. Reality itself demands an explanation.

7

Sensations and Reality

This world seems real because of its relationship to your senses. When you look at a house, you don't see it because it's there; it's there because you see it. If it were something to eat, you might taste it, smell it, see it, feel it, or even hear it. These are just ways to make you think it is real. It is the experience you go through that makes something exist. This world is one hundred percent subjective, rather than objective. That is, if a thing is not being experienced in any way by a form of life, that thing doesn't exist. Every particle of the earth is being experienced by certain of the heavens at all times, and this establishes the position of everything.

Even for your senses the basic principle is still knowledge compared to knowledge. Let's begin with the sense of taste. Four members of the Elect are involved in making the tastes.

What the Holy Ghost knows as an individual includes everything physical. This does not include thoughts, unless they have been spoken or written. There was a time and place where the Holy Ghost looked at all the trouble since Lucifer became a devil until the second coming of Christ.

The knowledge of all the trouble and evil of the last five thousand years can be apprehended by anyone so that he can experience it all, from a weak, barely discernible degree to one of great strength. All that is necessary is to taste anything bitter, for the one who is the Holy Ghost is also one of the four tastes. You are acquiring that knowledge through the sense of taste. Compared to your Heart of Man, it is bitter.

Emmanuel provides the taste of salt. It might seem fitting to think the Spirit of Love provides a sweet taste, but this is not so.

It is what another member of the Elect thinks of girls that causes this sensation.

The Spirit of Love had the job when she planned her life, of liking all people better than anyone else ever had. When you can see all of the shortcomings of the whole human race, this is a very difficult thing to do. The knowledge of her difficulty which she had while trying so to like people, that is the knowledge you receive when you taste anything sour. She is the spirit behind the lemon tree.

Adam was the first to have all four tastes. At the present time, each taste will bring up the inherited memory of how it seemed to your ancestors. This inherited memory will make up the largest part of the sensation of taste for you.

One member of the Elect is more sensitive to the four tastes and can detect them easier than anyone else. The part of the body of which he is in charge is the taste buds.

In the time before Adam, the human family could distinguish between tastes easily enough, but there was no knowledge connected with it, thus no sensation of taste. In regard to everything physical, the Elect have been on the job since the beginning. With Adam they began in everyone's mind. By combining the four tastes in different relationships and degrees with a few of the many odors, a wide variety of flavors can be produced.

Odors are knowledge acquired through the sense of smell. It might seem that when anything smells bad it is because it smelled bad to your ancestors, but this is only half true. There is one among the Elect whose job it is to determine everything that is poisonous by its smell. If people disliked everything that was bad, this would be an infallible way to detect poison. But if you like something that is not good, you might also like the smell of it, even though it is poisonous.

In the tastes of foods there is a third factor and an important one. As the colors in a painting are one thing but the painting something more, so the taste of food is more than a combination of the four tastes and smells. The taste also identifies the one who was the spirit of it while it was growing. One member of the Elect has the job of recognizing all the spirits behind food and imparting this knowledge. The stronger the taste, the further up he comes in your mind.

The first time you taste a food, you can tell more about it than you ever can again. The taste of cranberry sauce, for instance, gave some men the sensation of silliness. Other than the tastes and smells, you also get the knowledge of that member of the Elect who is the spirit behind it, and the spirit behind these berries is a princess who comes forward in the mind of every girl who likes to be foolish-minded about morals.

Moloch is the spirit behind the pepper plant. But the knowledge that goes with the taste is so covered by the inherited sensation of taste that few realize it is the knowledge of pain.

The Spirit of Love had certain work to do in a certain place where that work made the foundation for atoms. She represents the beginning. The work Emmanuel did there created the shape of the atoms; he represents the atom. The Holy Ghost is the one who is responsible for the molecule. And the one who is responsible for the crystal is briefly mentioned in the Bible as Melchizedek (or Melchisedec). The reason that this world apparently has form and weight is so involved, the subject will be taken up in the chapters dealing with atoms.

The same four are used to make the colors because of their part in creating the material side of this universe. Colors may not seem like knowledge, but they definitely are. Everyone's personality has a color to it. If you felt unselfish so often and strongly that unselfishness was your predominate feeling, this way of living would give the same sensation as bright yellow.

There was someone who had a vague but spiritual way of knowing things when he was a boy. He used this to see what harm it would do to other boys before he got into fights with them. This caused him to back out each time, because of his unselfishness. In commenting on this, someone else with spiritual understanding said, "He was not afraid; he was just yellow." Afterwards, it became common to associate the word *yellow* with fear. But this is a misnomer.

It is the Holy Ghost who provides the color yellow in the universe.

The Spirit of Love has to contend with evil so much that it was easy for her to provide black.

Life in its most wide-awake and vibrant form is red, a color which Emmanuel provides.

The color blue is the color of the personality of him who provides this color. For this one has lots of ambition and considerable ability, plus a strong appreciation of everything that would help bring happiness; but he planned his life so that he would never do much about it.

The color blue mirrors the personality of him who has it. Whenever anyone is feeling blue or melancholy, what he is feeling would produce the color of blue, if he could see it. When you look at the color of blue, you are acquiring through the sense of sight knowledge of a situation that would make you feel that way if you could feel it with greater intensity.

At birth the color of anyone's personality is the same as a white rose and stays that way until he enters the spirit of this world, or the spirit of this world enters him. When this happens to you, the expression of your eyes will change and your instincts will continue up to the last generation. After this, your personality is likely to begin changing color. Most adults have a personality color that is some shade of brown, caused by an acquisition feeling.

All other colors are made by combining the four basic colors in different ways. Combining red and yellow, for example, will make a color halfway between, which is orange. Red paint looks red because it absorbs all colors except red, which it reflects; yellow paint absorbs all colors except yellow, and so on. But if the red and yellow paint gave off their own lights so that they could be seen in the dark, then mixing these lights would make an orange color.

To modern man, colors are mostly an inherited memory from our ancestors of the sensation that the same colors gave to them. Thus, it would be possible to explain to a man who was born blind what a sunset looked like and get the idea across with a fair degree of accuracy. The amount of area each color occupied would have to be described, then a careful job of describing the feelings that each area represents would be necessary, so he could feel that situation in relation to his inherited memories. In that way his imagination would be controlled by inherited memories, and cause him to imagine what the sunset looked like.

Each of the four seasons has a separate feeling behind it. The Holy Ghost is the spirit behind fall. This is a husbandry feeling. It can be felt the strongest by someone who is feeling that the harvest is in for the winter. Any situation that will make a person feel he has managed some undertaking well will tend to make this feeling.

The Spirit of Love is the spirit of the winter, for both indoor and outdoor feelings. Children looking through a window at stormy weather outside, while they are standing in a warm room with happy games to play, are immersed in this spirit, as well as those who have a winter wonderland feeling caused by seeing a covering of snow.

The feeling of spring is really an ambitious feeling, but it will cause a feeling in some called spring fever, because the feeling of spring is more ambitious than the persons. When people can't keep abreast with this feeling, they want to lie down in a hammock. They will need something to make them work fast to get back into the spirit of spring.

Anyone can feel more ambitious in spring, if he has anything to feel ambitious about, but he can feel happy feelings easier in summer, if he has anything that makes a closer association with the Spirit of Truth through his inherited memories.

Youth, adulthood, middle age, and old age have the same spirits as spring, summer, fall, and winter, respectively.

These four also make the periods of the day. A morning feeling is very much like a spring feeling, but without its long-range type of ambition. Emmanuel is the time from noon till evening. This feeling is not as large in scope as summertime, but it is similar in type. The Holy Ghost is the time from evening till midnight. The Spirit of Love is the rest of the time until morning.

The same principle used in making all feelings is used to make the periods of the day, seasons of the year, and times of your life. The knowledge one gets as he begins one of these is a part of the personality of the one who is behind it. The part used is that which makes the desired feelings. For example, when you feel the personality of the Holy Ghost at evening time, it is the knowledge of fellowship feelings. This feeling has put many people in the mood to enjoy relaxing in an easy chair and talking, after the day's work is over.

The world should get pleasure and satisfaction from running industry, but it should be through with all business by noon. The afternoon should be for recreation, so that in the evening people could sit around and talk about it, among other pleasantries.

These days, the Spirit of Love seems very much asleep. In the time of Adam, the bottom of the first heaven was easily attainable. If you looked in that direction today, it would look so dark you would not realize you were looking at anything. An understanding of this hinges on an explanation of human minds.

Everyone has a carnal mind and a spiritual mind; actually, two sides of the same mind. Your soul and your mind are almost the same thing. One side of a soul is fastened to the body, the other to the first heaven. The side fastened to the body is called the carnal mind, the other the spiritual. It is something like a ship traveling close to shore where one side faces land and the other the sea, but it is *you* traveling through time with the first heaven and this world on either side.

It would be possible to go to sleep, then turn and walk out on the first heaven, the same as we normally walk in this world. Only now it is too dark to see. If people could do this now, their physical bodies would pass far more into an unconscious state than in ordinary sleep, and they would wake up perfectly refreshed.

In the days of Adam, this was called Paradise. There were good reasons why the path to Paradise should be hidden and remain so until the end of this age. In the Bible, the one in charge is called Michael. Any time this archangel stands up, the bottom of the first heaven will again become visible.

There is no danger of having too many people in it, for this universe is even more subjective and God even more infinite than anyone might think. If you looked at the farthest star you could see, and had a way of jumping out there and looking again, you would see just as many more stars each time you jumped. After a million jumps, you would have as many more to go before you reached the end as you had at the start. Astronomers can predict an eclipse far into the future, because all stars and planets obey very definite laws. Also, there are very definite laws at the microcosmic end of things.

If you had a way of becoming smaller and picked out something as small as you could see, to become that size yourself, in a few jumps you would soon be seeing crystals, then molecules. Yet the laws at this level make it possible to predict how elements will combine into compounds, always in the same proportions. In fact, laws are the only things that have been discovered. If you could go deep enough, into miniaturization, you would be involved in the laws of electricity and radio waves. Still, you would never find a solid particle, only laws.

Where there are laws, there must be an intelligence behind them. And such an intelligence would not be working without plan or purpose, for everything in the universe is completely planned.

This universe looks the way it would look if it existed, but it is only the plan of everyone's life that exists. All that gives these plans reality are feelings. A stick, a stone, a concrete road, all are made from feelings. Since the foundation for all feelings is knowledge compared to knowledge, then the feelings come from the world and the world comes from the feelings. The foundation of this world is nothing but a ghost, although a holy one. The Holy Ghost is that third of your soul which holds all of your inherited knowledge and memories.

If all human beings from the beginning to the second coming of Christ had had feelings only half as strong as they did, then this world would seem only half as real. It would be like walking around in a dream, half-conscious.

The reason the world seems real to lower forms of life is because it seems real to the spirit behind them. The feelings that are used to make heaven seem real are those felt by children below the age of accountability.

The feelings that were used to make the reality of this world include all types except profit feelings, and those of the young children. They include all kinds of pain and misery, all kinds of pleasure and happiness. The amount of feelings that people like compared to the ones they dislike is exactly the same. Since they are relative to each other, they have to be. These feelings mixed together make a strong enough world so that it seems real; but it is completely neutral, neither good nor bad.

If the world were made only out of miserable feelings, it would make anyone miserable just to be in it. But in a certain time, which the Bible calls "after the new Jerusalem," the world will be made out of only those feelings that people enjoy. If it were made out of these feelings now, it would seem very good to everybody just to be alive. For the reality of the world is made out of feelings that are automatically compared to your hereditary knowledge, and anything that is better than this will seem good to you.

Of course, if the world had always seemed this good, everyone's ancestors would have been so happy that now your inherited knowledge would have so much happiness in it that the world would again seem neutral. It would then be that much harder to make anything good enough to seem good.

So, until the end of this age the world needs wars, disease, crime, domestic troubles, accidents, and all kinds of misunderstandings. And to make these seem as bad as possible, you should try as hard as you can to prevent them. Trying hard to find the solution will also make you appreciate the truth all the more.

There are two reasons why the Bible doesn't tell all people to make themselves miserable on purpose. One is that people are not good enough to do it; the other is that if you try to make yourself miserable and do a good job of it, you would then feel satisfied. And you can't feel satisfied and miserable at the same time. If we were not coming near the end of this age which began with Adam, this would still need to be kept a secret.

If someone made a mistake and regretted it, the mistake itself might not result in good, but the regret of it would. Pain is disliked the most, of all feelings, but it is such an easy feeling to have that others are needed more. Misery in this world is not without purpose. As long as this world is in the age of work, this present age, there will be a need for miserable feelings to help make eternity better.

When you were planning your life before your birth, you could stop planning at this point where you are now, and find out what feelings were needed most, then plan out the rest of your life so that events would happen that would make you experience those particular feelings.

Although this world is planned, the plans can be changed if they are changed on the same level at which they are planned, and if the objective of doing it is right. When you planned out your life before you were born, that time is also now, because now is the same plans with some feelings added to make them seem real. At this time, before you were born, you had not planned out your future yet, so it would be a mistake to think that because the future is planned out you can't do anything about it. It may be planned out the way it is because you *did* try to do something about it.

Even though the world needs to feel much pain and misery until the end of this age, the time for this age to end depends on how people plan their lives.

To illustrate our condition: we are going along, and at one point we are born. Then we go on another inch, and at that point we die. But when we go on another fifty feet, we are just getting well started. The object of this one inch of present time is to make eternity as good as possible.

One way to see through this world is to do as a baby does when counting its fingers. Babies have been observed to keep track of something on their fingers, where each finger is a question and answer. Babies can remember the plans of their lives and know the future so easily that the natural question is, why is there so much pain, misery, and other trouble in the world?

The first finger is whether God is good or bad. They think God is good, and so the next question is whether God makes mistakes. The answer is, God makes no mistakes. The next question is, is God responsible for everything? The answer is, yes, because in the beginning there was nothing but God. The little finger is, What is the reason for all of this? The answer is,

Feelings are relative. For babies this kind of thinking is routine. If they continued on to their thumbs, this question would be, How does God think? This is the problem of infinity. If anyone began with his thumb, this question would be whether there is a God or not, but babies know more than that. Babies can look wiser than anybody.

Whether you go out in space or down into smallness, there is not only an infinite way to go, but God is even more infinite than that. A separate universe is created for each one who is born across the top of the first heaven.

Some people have two worlds created for themselves to begin with, as they are identical twins. Identical twins are just one person who is in two places at the same time.

The Bible states that the earth shall be inhabited in speaking of the hereafter. Because of this statement, some have wondered if the earth will be big enough for all people. However, there not only is a separate world for each human, but these worlds don't have to be synchronized with each other as they are today. Each person could have a whole world all to himself, if he wanted it that way. The difficult thing in this universe—which is taking so long to accomplish—is the work of getting feelings to the point where they will be as good as anyone would want them to be.

Everyone's world is synchronized with everyone else's, so that other people seem real enough, although they are just plans in your own world. However, the heavens of your universe are not always synchronized with everyone else's.

This gets back finally to the question of why Paradise will never have too many people in it. For if a whole army went there, it would seem to each man as though he were the only one who reached it, for the rest would be each in his own universe.

The thought of Paradise naturally brings up the feminine question, and its explanation also illuminates the homosexual problem. Most people consider the homosexual as someone who falls in love with a member of his own sex. When that happens, it is only the surface manifestation of something deeper. It is the deeper side, the fundamental causes, that should be understood.

8

Homosexual People

An article about inducting men into the army in the First World War told how the psychologists had difficulty separating some homosexual men who honestly believed they were not homosexual from normal men. They tried to act the way they thought men were supposed to act. This might make a person wonder what the word means, for there have been many homosexual people who have never fallen in love with any one of their own sex.

Besides a carnal mind and a spiritual mind, each of us has a conscious mind and a subconscious mind. All normal males have a subconscious mind that is feminine, and all normal females have a subconscious mind that is masculine. Our subconscious mind is better morally than our conscious mind.

Besides being in this world, you are also someone else's subconscious mind. As such, you are better than you are in this world, and for several reasons. Such as, you then possess no undesirable personality traits and are not influenced by evil spirits of any kind.

Your conscious mind is one-half of you; your subconscious mind is the other. When people plan their lives, they can plan to marry their own better half. Whether they do or not, this is the way it will be eventually. For a person's soul is made of the Spirit of Love, the Spirit of Truth, and the Holy Ghost. His better half has a soul made of the Spirit of Love, the Spirit of Truth, and the same Holy Ghost.

These three can be in as many places at the same time as is necessary for making souls. The Holy Ghost third of a soul has to be in only half as many places as the other two. So, there are only five parts for both you and your better half. It is impossible to spend eternity in the Holy Ghost with anyone else except the right one.

The time will come when each one will plan a happy lifetime for himself in this world, and after living that life he will go back and plan another. In those days it will become more important for the Holy Ghost to carry the instincts of husbands and wives together, than it now is, for everyone will marry the same one each time. Within each person's instincts there will be inherited memories that will make the one he marries seem like a part of himself.

Another reason why it is important that husbands and wives are made out of only five parts rather than two separate systems, is that this limitation puts them in each other's universe. So, the bottom of the first heaven is the same for both. In a future age, it will be possible for a married couple to leave this world together and live in a part of the first heaven for the rest of the night. In this present world, when a boy or girl sees his or her better half for the first time, the one observed may appear to stand out in relief in comparison with other people nearby, who may seem like mere images. This is because the two of them really are in the same world.

While every normal person has a subconscious mind of the opposite sex, there is a way for one's conscious and subconscious minds to trade places. Whenever this happens, he is then homosexual. The ones who turn this way may do so either quickly or slowly. When they turn slowly, they may be partly homosexual for a while but are not apt to stay this way very long.

Since the Holy Ghost holds each person's memories, as well as his instincts, and since there is only one Holy Ghost for each couple, a person's memories of his life on this world remain the same when he becomes homosexual. This fact would make it difficult for most people to tell what happened if they did become homosexual. But when a male becomes homosexual, his instincts are then feminine. When a female becomes homosexual, her instincts are then masculine.

Feelings can be used as handles to turn one into a homosexual. If a person knew how to do this on purpose, he could prevent it accidentally. Most cases could have been prevented at an early age.

The feelings used as handles are the prince and princess feelings. For example, there are certain fighting feelings that only boys and men—or girls and women who are homosexual in that way—can experience.

A prince was given the job of hunting down and eliminating a certain class of evil spirits that were bad for girls. He was given this job a few hundred years before he was born. By the time he was born, he had been trying to help girls for so long that he liked girls just because they were girls. This prince feeling is one of the easiest handles for girls to experience and hold. Yet girls can like other girls because they are friends or for other reasons, without doing any harm, no matter how long they are together. Any physical display of affection is usually headed off the right track, but it is the prince feelings that should be avoided.

Behind cursing and swearing there is a feeling that is not in a female's mind. When a woman or girl swears about anything, she is either feeling self-conscious—caused by her deliberate swearing—or is experiencing a homosexual feeling, or she learned cursing as part of the English language and uses the words the same as any other words. This last type usually talks easier and faster than most people. Some girls who feel self-conscious of their swearing may enjoy the feeling and not try to avoid swearing. There are other prince feelings that girls should shun, including anything characteristically masculine.

When boys become homosexual, it is usually started by getting a normal liking for each other associated with their looks. After that, any physical means of expressing affection is worse than for girls.

One of the things that everyone's subconscious mind has to do is fight diseases. This makes normal women more resistant to disease than men, because men are better at fighting.

One can go in a circle until one comes back to where one

started. This has been done many times in the universe. In the case of a married couple who are a part of each other, it can be arranged as a five-pointed star with one Holy Ghost position, two each of the Spirit of Love and Spirit of Truth positions. But there is another part of your being that is more important than any of these, and the rest of your being will need to be born into it some day. It is called the Holy Spirit.

9

Holy Spirit

The way a normal human being seems to himself derives from four parts. Besides the trinity of the soul, there is what the Bible calls the Holy Spirit. The knowledge of the Holy Spirit cannot be felt ordinarily because of the interference from both the spirit of this world and your own instincts. Otherwise, the Holy Spirit is just God who is the original source of all life; He is the spirit behind each of the Elect, and anyone else who is born across the top of the first heaven.

When a person is born, he does not yet have the Holy Spirit. This usually comes a few years later, but not until after the world has had a sufficient influence on the individual.

The Holy Spirit arrives through a direct line of all male ancestors for boys, or all female ancestors for girls. Before you receive the Holy Spirit, you receive your life through the parts of your soul.

I remember telling a certain person when I was very young that I had just hit this world with a thud. After it arrives, the Holy Spirit seems like yourself.

Emmanuel did not receive the Holy Spirit until he was baptized at the age of thirty. At that time he had still not been influenced by the spirit of this world, which is pride and death. Since there was also no hereditary interference, the Holy Spirit seemed like what it really was to him.

There are plain simple reasons why Emmanuel felt as he did during his crucifixion, for his feelings were caused by the same principle that explains everyone else's feelings.

For example, consider happiness and humor. No matter how happy a person was, if he could see inside his mind and see exactly why he felt happy, the feeling of happiness would leave while he was looking at it. He would then be merely looking at some spiritual mechanics in his own mind, and would no longer be feeling happiness because he would be seeing it instead. Sometimes, when something seems very funny, you will see exactly why it doesn't fit in your mind, if you look close enough. All the humor will then leave. The point is, you cannot feel that it doesn't fit while you are looking at *why* it doesn't fit.

While Emmanuel could see all the evil and sorrow in the world, he didn't have to feel it, only look at it. This condition lasted from the time he was baptized until near the end of his worldly life. But while he was being crucified he lost his ability to see everything, including the world's evil and sorrow, and then he had to feel this knowledge instead. This is the most anyone has ever felt in this world.

Before this time he could anticipate what was coming very intensely, because he understood it perfectly. When knowledge as bad as this is compared with something very good, it causes the Gethsemane-type of feeling. And in his case the Heart of Man was still as good as it had always been, for his life had no evil in it.

When Emmanuel thought of himself as separate from the Holy Spirit, he spoke as in Mark 10:18: "Why do you call me good? No one is good but God alone."

When Emmanuel spoke of himself as being with the Holy Spirit he spoke as in John 10:30: "I and my Father are one."

Being nailed to the cross caused a separation from the Holy Spirit. He could then no longer see all the evil and sorrow of this world, but after looking at it for three years he had this knowledge. It was this knowledge in comparison to his Heart of Man that caused the feelings he then had.

The way this feeling seemed could be described as depression, sadness, and despondency. This feeling became so strong it finally killed him; yet this is the feeling that all pleasure and happiness for eternity is based upon.

Because of the way feelings are relative, pleasure and happiness can be as good as this feeling was bad. This is mentioned in Heb. 12:2, "who for the joy that was set before him endured the cross."

Although God is the spirit behind a human being, all lower forms of life have a different spirit. The Elect themselves are the spirits behind most of the life born below the top of the first heaven. There is one Negro and one Chinese Elect. Although the Negro race at one time were on the same level as the whites and were born across the top of the first heaven, Lucifer had them sent back down. Instead of taking individual responsibility in coming across the first heaven, the Negroes ganged on the devil.

If you hit the devil before you were born, you would be born with curly hair, whether any of your ancestors had had curly hair or not. To kick the devil would make very curly hair. To do this with very strong feelings would make kinky hair.

Each member of the Elect, except a few at the top, has a demon. These demons are in everyone's mind. When someone commits a heinous crime, he is not alone in it. The reason he commits the crime is that he likes how it makes him feel. There is usually considerable pride mixed with it, but the special feeling in causing the crime is the one that brings up a knowledge of all other crimes of like nature.

If you had lived on this earth a few centuries ago, you probably would not believe radio and television were possible. But you would believe in demonology and witchcraft then, because you would have to contend with them.

There are a number of beings besides the Elect who walk into your mind, bringing their knowledge which makes you have their feelings. Instead of living in your body as the Elect do, they live in the unconscious body of the angel from the third heaven. They live in the spirit of this world, they live in pride, they live in death. Whenever you experience any of these feelings, you get them through that part of your body to which Lucifer (as a member of the Elect) has always been connected, the thyroid gland.

Death hangs between this world and hell in a certain spiritual order of things, but the top of death is very close to this world. A host of demons live here.

Merlin, a prophet and magician, made a hinge by which it was possible to open a door to this underworld from our world. The tall stones that were used and are still standing in England are at a site called Stonehenge, originally "stone hinge." This had to be made at a place where many people entered death together. Before that, Stonehenge was used as a place of worship, offering human sacrifices.

In the days when idols were worshiped intensely, there was an idol of revenge where people worshiped who were calling for vengeance on someone. There was also an idol of jealousy. These two were later placed in the spirit of this world.

Whenever anyone feels one of these feelings, a part of his mind is coming close to this idol. Nothing in this world is ever lost. Everything that ever happened and every thought ever thought is still in the same place. We have just moved along in time. The worship which these idols received when they were in this world was placed with the idols, and everyone who goes there receives this knowledge. To feel jealousy or revenge is to commit idolatry.

The way demons receive their feelings is just the opposite from human beings. The condition you are in will feel good if it is better than your Heart of Man, to which it is compared. For demons, their condition remains constant, but it is compared to the feelings of the world, and to the misery of any particular trouble they have caused. If everyone felt good, the demons would be miserable; but if everyone became miserable the demons would feel very elated.

In this world, demons appear as feelings, and they are feelings to the people who experience them. When you do what a demon tells you to do, it will cause you to enter the spirit of this world to some degree, which causes a certain amount of pride, in addition to sharing the pleasure of the demon that led you to commit the misdeed. For many types of crime it will cause a high degree of pride, but there are many small, everyday matters about which demons try to influence you. Practical jokes they use as a wedge.

In many cases, you vaguely sense that you want to do some particular thing for no apparent reason. Some people almost invariably ask the wrong questions. The people who do this on purpose enjoy these demon feelings. They ask questions until they hear something that insults someone, then make sure the insulted one hears about it. Demon feelings are especially strong in vandals.

The prince of demons is named Gog, and he can make you feel very important. The closer to the front of your mind he comes, the more important you will feel.

When you try to do what you wish when the feeling is caused by a demon, you are then "giving heed to deceitful spirits and doctrines of demons" (1 Tim. 4:1).

Demons are ordinary-looking fellows in the back of your mind who try to tell you what to do. They are not compelled to tell the whole truth, and what they do say is calculated to cause harm. However, one reason demons exist is that they say they do. So, if a demon becomes a liar, he eliminates himself. Even so, demons are extremely misleading.

The closer to your consciousness a demon comes, the easier you can know whatever the demon knows. In this case, it is like looking into your own knowledge for the facts. When a demon comes too far he can't prevent you doing it.

Some persons have allowed a demon to come so far up into their minds at certain times that the demon could look out onto this world. When a demon does this, it makes windows out of the person's eyes, but a window works both ways—you can also see in.

When a person is looking at you at the same time a demon is, it will create a gleaming look in the back of the person's eyes, like looking into a bright room where you can't see anything except the brightness. If the demon stops looking at you while the person is still looking, the brightness will instantly disappear. If the demon uses a person's eyes for windows and looks at you while the person is looking elsewhere, you will note a hard, glittering look in the person's eyes.

This is not the kind of shine caused by feeling proud, although some people are so big spiritually that their eyes shine or even gleam when they feel proud, if they are observed by someone much smaller. Making sacrifices when you plan out your life will make you bigger spiritually. Whether you are big or small, your feelings will still seem the same to you. Children at Christmas may have eyes that glow with happiness and excitement, but that is yet another look.

Many people have observed strange and eerie things that can be accounted for only by the existence of demons. A demon must be the spirit behind something on this world in order to be here. Each of the demons is the spirit behind an insect family.

Although all demons will someday be done away with, there is a spiritual reason for insects other than that fruit trees and flowers depend on them for pollination. When the time comes when there will be no more demons, God will be the spirit behind all insects.

The spiritual reason for insects is to make the world seem more real. If you walk around a corner and suddenly see a mountain not too distant and if the mountain was not being experienced by life in any form except yourself, you would sense a feeling of unreality to it, like a painted picture presented for you to see. If the Holy Spirit, who seems like a part of yourself, was experiencing the mountain through many other beings besides yourself, then it would also seem more real to you.

The ideal beings for experiencing the material side of this world should have many legs, many eyes, and be very numerous. This is one of the fundamental reasons for insects, and when the time comes for God to be the spirit behind all insects, this world will seem more real than it had ever seemed before.

Trying to make this world seem real is one of the main functions of creation. For a god with nothing but an unlimited mathematical ability, one who thought of numbers as amounts and could think in a way that would keep track of an unlimited number of amounts, he could create a universe like this one. He would also have to separate himself so that he could look at his own mathematics without understanding them. If it were arranged so that certain combinations would give certain impressions passed from generation to generation, the time would come when all of mathematics would be seen only as symbols. Everything that was seen would then be an illusion. And that is what this world is.

If anyone were going to try to understand the principles that make up the illusion of this world, he would need to know that each of the Elect is in each third of his mind or soul, so that each of the Elect must create three different feelings. Each third of your soul looks like your body, but each has only the one spirit. In this world all three are in the same place.

In most cases, feelings complement each other. For example, a strong feeling of bravery is caused by pushing just as strongly against fear. Where there is no fear or wanting to get away, there can be no bravery. The one who can feel fear the strongest can also feel bravery the strongest.

The feeling of peace can be much stronger and more enjoyable than most people realize. This feeling is Emmanuel coming up in the Spirit of Love third of your soul. When he drove the money changers out of the temple, this was a feeling contrary to peace. When you feel this type of indignation, it is Emmanuel coming up in the Holy Ghost third of your soul. When you aim at the truth strong enough to feel it, you then are going higher in Emmanuel's third of your soul.

The Holy Ghost is more sensitive to worldly feelings than anyone esle. These are the feelings that you pick up from other people who are feeling them. They include all crime and every kind of domestic bickering, which interfere with all good feelings. He has the strongest dislike of worldly feelings. When you experience this feeling of dislike with the world, it is he, coming up in the Spirit of Truth third of your soul. He can't do anything about this, so he doesn't try. When you feel complacent, it is he coming up in the Spirit of Love third of your soul. But when you feel fellowship, it is he coming into his own.

If you try to help someone where your motive is the Spirit of Love, and if your attempt at helping meets with rebuff, this situation will produce a feeling. Young children feel rebuffed very often. When you feel it, it is the Spirit of Love coming up in the Holy Ghost third of your soul. The Spirit of Love also abhors evil. When you feel this, it is she coming up in the Spirit of Truth third of your soul. But when you try to help someone or try to make someone happy, and want it strong enough to feel it, it is the Spirit of Love coming into her own.

The way many of the Elect were able to have feelings arrayed in opposites was to start out in the first part of their lives with one kind of feeling, then later change to feeling the opposite.

The one who had the job of making reckless feelings in the universe experienced these before he became grown. This one got a job driving a truck in his adult life. By that time he had learned to control his reckless feelings, and his run included snowy, mountainous roads. When you feel careful, it is he coming up in one part of your soul, and when you feel reckless, it is he again in another part.

The name of one position is satire. The one who holds it was the smartest in school, but she used it to make sarcastic remarks about everyone else. In later life she did the opposite and used the most anxious thoughtfulness in considering how things were going to sound before she said them.

The one who likes teamwork the best, as in a football game, is also the one who brings up the knowledge of every situation where anyone felt he was alone. Some who have been taken out early in the morning and hanged have felt the most alone.

Sometimes the feelings will help make each other stronger without being opposite. For example, the one who makes sick feelings is also the melancholy feeling.

There is a feeling to being a mother; that is one of the feelings Emmanuel's mother makes. The other two go with praying and mercy. A man can have these feelings to some extent, but less than a woman.

Every worthwhile way to strengthen feelings in this universe has been used, including the principle of killing two birds with one stone. The spirit of hunting is also he who was given the job of hunting down evil spirits that were bad for girls. Doing this not only made him like girls better; it made him like hunting better.

There is not room in the front of your mind for many feelings at the same time. The farther front they come, the less room there is. Sometimes the one who is excitement will come up so far that not even pain can be felt at the same time. When the one who is excitement is at the front of your consciousness, you then have the knowledge of all exciting situations, the same as that member does.

How does a member of the Elect make you have his or her knowledge by coming up to the front of your mind? The answer is, instead of you being a simple individual you are really made out of the entire Elect with yourself in front; you are unaware of the rest until one or more come up far enough to make you aware of them. In that case you have their knowledge for nearly the same reason you have your own, for they are part of you.

There is the question of whether God is three different feelings and appears in three different ways, but here the situation is reversed. As all other members of the Elect have a place in the Spirit of Love, the Spirit of Truth, and the Holy Ghost, so also do these three have a place in God.

When you feel holy, if you continue in this direction it is like going into a large vacuum. Go in the opposite direction far enough and you will see everything in the universe. The first place in God, where holy feelings are, is for the Holy Ghost, and the second is for Emmanuel. The Spirit of Love position has been adopted as the one through which all dealings with the human family will take place.

No matter what God does or thinks, no member of the Elect comes into God's mind at that level except the Spirit of Love. This is why the names God and Love have become confused. Love is a state of mind. God is life.

Even the most unusual of the Elect still have much in common with the rest. Emmanuel, for example, has a subconscious mind. As explained, the subconscious mind of a man is feminine. The Lord's bride is the one who brings you the knowledge of all the happiness in the universe. This in turn will make you recall from your inherited memories how happiness felt to your ancestors. A closer association with the Spirit of Truth and the feeling of happiness mean more to her than to anyone else; she is also the spirit of the church. The Lord's bride was born during this present century, as were many others, including the Spirit of Love.

Among the unusual ones would be the Spirit of Love. An interesting feature would be her birth and how things were for her parents. At an early age her father had to act in a certain way that made him unique, as Emmanuel's mother is.

Many young children can retain certain feelings and allow those feelings to control them. If the feelings are ones that help in playing musical instruments, then anyone who can be obedient to these feelings is called musically gifted. Very young children sometimes can have the Spirit of Love feeling strong enough to let it tell them what to do, and they may hold on to this feeling for several days at a time. In one case a boy had the Spirit of Love feeling and held it until he grew up and got married. He was the only one ever to do this. Strong inherited memories from his ancestors were mixed in his marital relations, and they jarred him loose from the control of the Spirit of Love. Until that time the Spirit of Love was responsible for everything in his life.

What puzzled his wife about the birth of their oldest daughter was that three months before the daughter's birth her own hips began to grow wider, and three months after her birth they had returned to normal. It was this way also with Emmanuel's birth and for those in Adam's time, until the people took Lucifer's advice. There was no pain or discomfort in these births. This is the way it will be in the future.

The oldest daughter of this marriage is she who has the Spirit of Love position on the Elect, and it was she who had been controlling her own father for so long. There was no egg involved in her conception, but for Emmanuel there was nothing but an egg. Her position on the Elect is greater than Emmanuel's, for the same reason that the Spirit of Love is greater than the Spirit of Truth.

Few of the Elect are mentioned in the Bible. One who was mentioned is Mammon. If you acquire enough money or wealth and think about it enough to feel rich, that feeling is he. However, for most of his life he was anything but rich. So, he also creates an opposite type of feeling. A rich feeling is being made into a good one for eternity, but right now it interferes with acquiring wisdom.

The name of one position is the hero. If you should do something that was a help to people, and if others had tried and failed, you can then very easily feel a hero. To feel it the strongest, you should not think anything that would minimize your own importance in what you did.

The hero also desires to make a good impression; this is one of the three feelings he creates. This is not a feeling of pride, but it is the closest thing to it.

If the Elect were lined up in rank, according to which personality was the closest to pride, then the hero, whose name is St. Peter, would be the first, and Emmanuel would be the last. From a certain view they would have the appearance of gold-colored bricks or stairs. Where St. Peter is the gate, Emmanuel is the way.

After the judgment, everyone who is going to live forever is going to have to go through the Elect. Those who do not qualify to live forever will not be able to get past St. Peter. Those who do can keep going; when they pass Emmanuel, they will be on their way.

The most important lineup of the Elect is the one used in creation, where the Holy Ghost is number two, the Spirit of Love is number three, et cetera. In this order the last active member is number 665 and has a position called the worm. If you think in a certain way that makes you tell someone "what's what," then walk away with the belief that you are right, without giving the person a chance to answer, the feeling that goes with it is brought up in your mind by the worm. Also, when you discover you have made a mistake and feel compelled to go back and apologize, the crawling-back feeling you will have is also caused by the worm.

Creating feelings as good as anyone would want them to be without causing any unnecessary trouble is so complicated that when each person planned his life, the Elect helped with what influence they had, beginning with number one. The Holy Spirit acts something like a guy wire that gives a constant pull in the right direction, even though it is easy to resist. The Holy Ghost with his fellowship is next. The Spirit of Love is next; it's what the world needs now. Next is the Spirit of Truth whose help lies in discovering the truth. Next is the Intermediary whose feeling is that he wants everything right. And then all the rest in that order.

If the plans of the world had gone by the Elect beginning at the lightweight end, they would have gone off the track with each step. Yet the time is coming when there will be no need for trouble of any kind, and everyone will be as good as he is supposed to be. It will be easy enough then for the rest to follow with the lightweight end of the Elect in front.

When time ends and eternity begins, this will be accomplished by turning time around, which in turn will be done by turning the direction of the Elect around. Instead of the worm following, he will turn and go the other way. But many things must happen before the worm turns.

To discuss all the hundreds of the Elect would take an enormous book. An even more important reason not to discuss each one is to help keep their identities a secret. Many of them tried to plan out their lives so they would not know who they were themselves, although they may have experienced some puzzling things of a mental nature. Experimenting with things of a spiritual nature should be avoided. No matter how puzzling anything of a mental nature may seem, it always has a logical explanation, as in the case of my uncle, who could tell all about a gun by looking at the bullet hole caused by the gun firing accidentally.

There is a special feeling connected with the handling of a gun. With this feeling you will always remain conscious of the direction the gun is pointing, and eliminate gun accidents. The member of the Elect who makes this feeling is also the one behind the feeling of an accident. If you had an accident caused by a gun accidentally discharging, the one who instills the feeling of an accident would know what kind of gun it was, since he was there in your mind when it happened. And he, of course, is the uncle earlier mentioned. Seeing the bullet hole enabled him to get hold of that particular accident in his mind.

In order to make this world seem as real and materialistic as possible, there needed to be in your inherited memories things just the opposite, so that your worldly experiences by comparison would seem more real. After your ancestors acquired the necessary experience with the supernatural, it needed to be eliminated.

The universe had to be made so that it would seem like something physical and solid, not something vague and spiritual.

The competent and confident executive feeling, number six, is also the materialist. He tried to make this world seem real and eliminate all the phantoms and everything supernatural. He worked at this for so long before he was born that when he finally came to this world, he liked everything of a material nature. This feeling will make a person like machinery, just because it is machinery. When anyone does not have his mind set against this feeling, it will make him like buildings, boats, airplanes, or anything of a material nature.

When one is young and can easily make up his mind and is then forced to contend with mechanical problems, he might never like anything of a mechanical nature. There have been many who have decided they don't like to confront mechanical problems and have thought it so firmly their minds remained that way the rest of their lives. Trying to invent anything will always produce a drudgery feeling for them.

Yet this entire universe is an invention, although very complicated and hard to fathom. Whatever you see with your eyes can also be seen another way under certain conditions, as in sleepwalking.

A man once described everything as seeming very bright when he was walking in his sleep on a dark night. There are a few cases on record of people, usually children, who experience this while still awake. With eyes shut or blindfolded, they can read or recognize cards put in front of them. This is like looking inside to see instead of outside. The highest level at which this could be done would be as it looked to Paul on the road to Damascus. Such miracles might be categorically denied by an atheist, but an understanding of the principles behind the creation of this universe shows them to be logical.

The best argument in favor of atheism I can find is that "there is no God, because if there is a God, where is He?" Anyone who could see well in the dark might have a hard time opening his eyes against a bright light, as in a poem by Coleridge in which the atheist Ole came out of his dark hiding place at noon and with eyes shut looked up at the sun and hooted, "Where is it?"

The spiritual machinery behind all of creation can be very complicated, but it is not necessary to understand how this universe was created in order to get the most good out of it for eternity. It would have been very easy to plan this world so that everyone would be rich in material things. The cost of war alone would have made everybody rich. The big problem, however, was to make feelings become as enjoyable as anyone would want them to be.

In the age of happy times, everything that is good will seem good, because it will be compared to something in the Lord's House that is the opposite. Therefore, it is desirable for everyone to acquire the skills for doing everything in a way that will result in the most pleasure and happiness.

When each one planned his life for this present world and there was something good to be gotten for himself, then one way to get it for eternity was to sacrifice it during this lifetime. Some could have attained much happiness from music and also made considerable money from it, but they sacrificed it instead. Everything else that is any good has also been sacrificed, including marriage. However, it is too difficult for everyone to get everything this way, so the principle of all for one and one for all is used here. It is like everyone giving all he has to God and having the entire amount given back to each separately.

Instead of the entire world putting all the skills that have been sacrificed, and everything else that is any good, all in one unit, each team individually has to do this.

When it comes to possessing these things, you can have as much as you can forgive. The meaning of the word *forgiven* can seem very puzzling. It is the words "given for" turned around. If one boy takes another's bicycle to ride without asking, and if the owner gives him permission to ride after the ride is over, then when the permission was "given for" the ride, he was forgiven.

If someone does something you dislike very much and if you forgive him for it, you are giving him permission for the past deed. It is easy to say you forgive someone and to fool yourself in the process. The amount of forgiveness you need depends on your understanding of each situation that requires it. The more understanding you have, the less forgiveness you need and still do a complete job of forgiving. The reason is that everyone has a perfect excuse for everything he ever did he should not have done.

The trouble with excusing yourself in this way is that if you are going to hell, you have a perfect excuse for going there, and if you are going to be done away with and go back to where you were before you were created, you have a perfect excuse for being that way, too. Everything you ever did left its effect on yourself. So, if you argue that you had a perfect excuse for staying drunk, breaking your leg, or whatever, the answer to that is, what of it? For the thing itself is where the trouble is.

Some people do more good than others, but that may be because they have more intelligence, ambition, unselfishness, or other assets which help them do more. To whom much is given, much is expected.

Some people have stronger desires and a greater capacity for happiness than average. However much happiness you can hold, that is what you will get. But at the moment you would not trade places with the next one above you, because then you would have to do more, and you would not trade places with the next one below you, because then you would not receive as much. You pick your own place.

To live a lifetime in the days of the new Jerusalem will be very good, but even so you can improve it. That is because the Spirit of Truth owns all pleasure and happiness; the Holy Ghost has the power to give power, including the giving of all skills;

and the Spirit of Love is the ticket. When anyone tries to help anyone else hard enough to feel it, this will result in something the Spirit of Love can see, the ticket, and when big enough, she takes it. She gives this to the Holy Ghost, and he uses this to give you more of whatever kind of skill or ability you want. When you use a skill or ability with the right motive, the Spirit of Truth adds the pleasure and happiness that goes with it.

The more pleasure and happiness the Spirit of Truth gives away, the more enjoyment he has himself, but he can't give it away without a reason. The Holy Ghost owns all the skills, ambitions, and abilities. The more he gives away, the more enjoyment he has, also; but he can't give you any more ability than you naturally develop without a ticket.

Acquiring more ability is desirable, except in those who are going back to where they were before they were created, to the point where they cease to exist. So, it becomes more important to establish the fact that you are going to live forever than to learn anything else.

In many places in the Scriptures it is stated that anyone who believes Emmanuel is what he is will have eternal life, as in John 3:15. "That whoever believes in him may have eternal life."

If a person waited until a time like the Judgment, when he can see who's who and then believe, his belief will do him no good. For his faith will have to come while he is living in the spirit of this world, before his belief can save him from it, because the spirit of this world is also death.

Only Emmanuel has a direct connection to life through death itself. This makes him our only way out of death, for death is also a place, and we are in it now. The direct connection that Emmanuel has with life is made possible by his unique heredity. The subconscious mind of Emmanuel's mother, called the better half, was Joseph, her husband. If Joseph and his forefathers had been different, then some of Emmanuel's masculine characteristics would also have been different, even though he acquired them in a roundabout way. All of this was necessary to eliminate any future interference between himself and the Holy Spirit.

To believe Emmanuel is who he is, while you are still of this world, is to turn over a certain amount of control to the Spirit of Truth third of your soul from the Holy Ghost third. The way to turn over more control is to not only believe but to live according to your belief. The Holy Ghost third of your soul is where all of your memories are, as well as all of your instincts; so it is the main thing that makes you different from anyone else.

If one has come back from the grave and convinced me that Emmanuel was the Spirit of Truth, then my belief would not be based either on my own ability to aim at the truth or anyone else's; this would have done no good. If you believe without being forced to, this would guarantee that you would live forever.

To estabilsh a connection with the Spirit of Truth through all of your memories and instincts in order to live forever, it is not necessary to aim at the truth so that you can know anything you wish, only well enough to know Emmanuel for what he is. If you can, you will be here during the age when it will be as easy to go in and out of this world as it sounds in John 10:9 where Emmanuel says, "I am the door: by me if any man enter in, he shall be saved, and shall go in and out, and find pasture."

Of the many things to enjoy for eternity that we are paying for during this age, the most enjoyment will be had from marriage. Each member of your team will be in many places at the same time. When you are in many places at the same time, no two of you would need to look alike. If you were talking to any one of yourselves, it would seem no different than if you were talking to someone else.

Your better half will be in the same number of places that you are in. You will plan your life to marry the same one each time you marry. Each time you will have two children, a boy and a girl. Brothers and sisters will not marry each other, but each time you marry it will be to your better half.

This coming age of complete happiness, with no pain or trouble of any kind, the Bible calls the new Jerusalem.

10

New Jerusalem

The word *city* in the Bible sometimes means a large worldly feeling created by the many people involved in it. In looking over a modern large town or city, it seems that the term should be "organized confusion." The name the Bible gives the spirit behind it is Babylon.

This spirit of many people feeling pride is called Tyrus. This is described in the twenty-sixth, twenty-seventh, and twenty-eighth chapters of Ezekiel; the king of Tyrus is Lucifer. The spirit of this world is sometimes called the sea. This sea, with all the feelings it makes, will need to be removed.

In the days of the new Jerusalem the city itself is created by the feelings of all its people. With no unhappiness of any kind and with the feelings of enjoyment increased many times, this creates the situation described in Rev. 21:1, 2: "Then I saw a new heaven and a new earth; for the first heaven and the first earth had passed away, and the sea was no more. And I saw the holy city, new Jerusalem, coming down out of heaven from God, prepared as a bride adorned for her husband."

Every time this world runs its complete course it can be rerun, but never again will there have to be another Lord's House built. What is being built now will be used again each time, so there will be no need for a devil, demons, or any form of trouble.

Where pride now causes an object to be valued highly, there will be better reasons. The spirit that is created by people having strong feelings, can not only be felt by other people, but the spirit can become attached to objects. When you enter an empty church, it feels like a church; an empty schoolhouse feels like a schoolhouse. A piece of furniture that has remained in a happy home for a long time will have a slight happy feeling attached to it. If you were surrounded by these antiques they could make you aware of it.

There are old houses in England in which a family must have been filled with hate for so many years that it ended in murder. No family can live there for long now, because they can't stand the feelings. The new Jerusalem will have no hate feelings. But some antiques will become quite valuable.

The physical aspects of the world will be somewhat different from what they are today. The explanation also makes clear why tropical flowers have been found frozen in the ice in the far north, why elephant-like animals have been dug out of the ice in Alaska and Siberia, where they had frozen so rapidly and without ever again thawing that the meat was still good to eat after thousands of years.

To understand the reason clearly, one should understand the characteristics of a greenhouse. While it is true that the glass of a greenhouse holds the warm air in, and that is the main reason for its effectiveness, it is also true that the shorter rays of the heat spectrum are more penetrating than the longer rays. Short heat rays from the sun penetrate the glass, while the long rays from the earth are reflected. The right humidity and atmospheric conditions will do the same thing as the glass. On a clear frosty morning the earth has radiated much of its surface heat out into space, but if there were a layer of clouds to reflect the heat back to earth, it would not have been so cold.

In desert lands where the air is dry it gets very cold at night, despite a hot daytime temperature. Water holds heat so well that if the air had been saturated with moisture, it would have stayed warm all night.

If there were some way to remove all snow and ice from the world and put enough moisture into the atmosphere and hold it there until the sun could warm up the surface of the earth, as well as all the moisture in the air, this condition would stay that way of its own accord. The atmosphere would act like the glass in a greenhouse. The warmer air is, the more moisture it will hold, so there would be nothing to make this condition unstable.

There is much evidence to indicate that the world was once much hotter than now. As the planet cooled, there was plenty of moisture in the air to produce the greenhouse effect. As soon as the earth's temperature moderated enough to support life, life began to manifest itself in material form. All material things are made of life. An electron microscope will show that some viruses are apparently molecules without life, except under certain conditions; then they become violently alive.

In the days of Adam there was an overcast around the entire world. This also reflected the sunlight to the extent that the earth never got totally dark at night. In the daytime the sun could not be seen; only a brightness in the sky.

At night the earth never had time to cool, for the air was damp and warm, and the earth could not radiate its heat through the overcast. Under these conditions, there was no problem in obtaining food, clothing, or housing. All land had a mildly tropical climate, and the Garden of Eden was the whole world. In those days there could be a fine mist, but there were no rain, snow, hail, or storms of any kind.

When the new Jerusalem begins, the material reality of the world will be made up of all the feelings people will then have from the beginning of that age until its end. However, instead of the good feelings being balanced by the bad, there will be nothing but enjoyable feelings.

Every experience that anyone has will be compared to something of an opposite nature in the Lord's House. The comparison will make the world itself seem very enjoyable. Everything of a negative nature, both physical and mental, will have been eliminated, including the self-hypnotizing way of making up your mind so strongly when young that it stays that way the rest of your life. Many people are now in some kind of mental straitjacket and have no idea that their trouble began in years of infancy.

But when this world runs over again, there will be nothing holding anyone back. Scientific discovery, experimentation, and invention can give so much pleasure and enjoyment that even though little work will be necessary in that kind of climate, there will be much more accomplished materially than at present. Before people die of old age, they will be able to talk to God again, just as when they were very young.

Even with unbounded happiness, however, one unfulfilled desire will continue to increase from one generation to the next; that is, everyone will want to see God. They will want God to manifest himself in a physical form so they can see him with their eyes. The people will be told to prepare for His coming, and when they are ready, God *will* be revealed in a physical form.

The people will then build the right kind of houses on high enough ground; they will store up food and make other preparations. When all is ready, a very large meteorite will land in the sea where it will do no damage. It will let in the cold from outer space, causing the moisture in the air to condense around the hole made by the meteorite's entrance. As the moisture condenses, it will lower the pressure which in turn will lower the temperature. This will cause more moisture to condense, so there will be a curtain of rain shaped in the form of a circle. This circle will continually enlarge. The meteorite will merely trigger something that was ready to go. This ring of rain will spread until it covers the entire world. When it stops raining, the immediate result will be an atmosphere that is dry and cold.

When the people then look at the night sky, which they will see for the first time in their lives, they will see stars as far as their telescopes can probe. The size of this universe can be appreciated best on a clear, starry night. They will know then that they are looking at infinity in a physical form, and that is God in physical form!

With adequate telescopes, other instruments, and accurate star maps, it will be possible after centuries of study to prove how God thinks. The work that the angels of the third heaven do is arranged to explain infinity.

After Lucifer made a devil of himself, the world did not remain in the antediluvian age very long. There was a spiritual arc made between this world and a division of the second heaven, which is on a different time plane. The object was to save the right kinds of life from the earth before the rains came. This was Noah's undertaking.

From the third heaven a planet about the same size as ours was brought in close to the earth at such high speed that it sailed on past into space again. As it went by, it attracted a chunk of the earth that tried to follow it, but the other planet was going too fast. This chunk is now the moon. The disturbance to the world caused by the moon breaking away was so great that it broke the crust of the earth under the seas, creating vast lava beds there.

In those days, there were seas that boiled and land upheavals of every kind. Some ocean floors were raised to where the oceans drained and evaporated, leaving only salt domes and pools of fish oil many feet deep.

With the earth and the moon trying to adapt to their proper orbits, the unsettled condition of the earth remained that way for some time. Earthquakes caused large sections of ground to slide for miles, covering up the pools of fish oil under a layer of earth thousands of feet deep.

In the antediluvian age before the rains came, there was no danger of forest fires, for the humidity was always high and there was no lightning. The floor of a forest would continually thicken as trees would fall over, and other trees would grow over them. A forest floor would evolve over many millions of years into thick composted layers of leaves, needles, dead wood, and all kinds of vegetation.

At the time the moon was torn away and the earth was readjusting itself to roundness once again, thick layers of earth slid sideways, covering up a primeval forest with a floor over a thousand feet thick. This was compressed under such high pressure that the air trapped in it became very hot. Without enough oxygen to burn, it carbonized all the vegetable matter. The higher the pressure, the harder the coal it produced.

When the life that was saved was put back on the world, it found itself in a very different environment. The best of the human family were saved; the rest were destroyed, giving the human family a much better start. In the years that followed, there was a split in the human family. There had to be much industry and hard work for those who emigrated north. The other part went south. These never had to make much industrial progress, and so little was made. Under a constant hot sun the people acquired a darker skin that was passed on in the hereditary process, and their spiritual escapades kinked their hair. Those who went north had to find how to preserve food for the winter, as well as how to make houses and clothes that were warm enough, forcing faster progress on the human family. When the industrial age arrived, oil fields and coal beds were available to help speed progress. By speeding up the industrial development of the world, the inventive ability of the average person and his familiarity with things mechanical and scientific were increased.

Today, the world feels proud of its industry and military strength. So many are feeling proud that a strong spirit is created.

When a world war starts, there are enough feelings generated to create a spirit that others can feel and make them want to join in. The more people join, the larger a war spirit becomes; and the larger it becomes, the more people are influenced to join. In a small military contest between the United States and Russia, control of the size could be lost very fast. Yet neither side wants any of the possessions of the other. It would simply be a killing war.

Pride can not only make people want to fight, but the political problems involved are kept unsettled by pride more than any other thing.

There are answers to how to have peace, and a desire to know the truth will cause a feeling that could show the way to peace. But other untoward feelings will interfere.

Feelings generally have minds of their own. When some people claim they hear voices in their own minds, they really do. Demons especially are a noisy bunch.

When this contest comes to a head, there will be an end to

it called Armageddon. It has been going on since Adam's time as stated in Eph. 6:12: "For we wrestle not against flesh and blood, but against principalities, against powers, against rulers of the darkness of this world, against spiritual wickedness in high places."

Demons are forever trying to get as much control of each individual as possible, and one way is by actually helping that individual. The more help you accept from demons, the more you come under their influence.

Some people allow a demon to come so close to their consciousness that they can know certain information because the demon knows it. These people know they have a mysterious source of knowledge, even though they don't understand it, or the implications of their bondage.

When a member of the Elect comes forward in your mind, he brings knowledge of only one subject but a colossal amount of it. When a demon is near enough for you to feel his knowledge, you might learn things that are helpful, but you should expect him to try to fool you. As it states in 1 John 4:1, "Beloved, believe not every spirit, but try the spirits whether they are of God: because many false prophets are gone out into the world."

A few adults can indeed talk to God directly, but they have acquired the ability under such responsibility that they do not have the right to ask for help for themselves or for others. If other people get through to Him by prayer, they are earning their right to be heard. Prayer has interference from a long line of instincts, going back to God.

The end will come after everything worth having has been paid for. It would be good if future tribulation did not have to happen, but the human experiences that are so bad they make the opposite kind seem good by comparison are not there unless they are experienced.

Getting the benefits from all the trouble the world has ever had must be accomplished in three ways, because there are three parts to your soul. For the Spirit of Love portion you will give God all that you earned, and God will give back all that the entire team has earned. For the Holy Ghost segment the way to receive is based on forgiveness. When a person does harm to you, that harm is used to make feelings better. When you forgive, you receive the good; but if you don't forgive him, he receives it. Involved is a position of the Elect called justice. This Elect will earn everything for himself by going through the same experiences others had when they earned it.

He who is justice will not forgive anyone, for he cannot; it is not his function to. Likewise, the top four (God, the Holy Ghost, the Spirit of Love, and the Spirit of Truth) are not going to forgive the one who is justice, either. When justice does not forgive you, you not only receive everything that justice owns, but you also will have to pay back every cent you ever received to which you were not justly entitled.

When a person receives everything that justice has to give because justice did not forgive him, justice then receives the same amount back from the top four, because they did not forgive justice; so he has to give it all to the next one.

In order for justice to tolerate it when God does not forgive, justice had to contend with demons with no help from the Holy Spirit during his entire life. To survive when the Holy Ghost does not forgive him, he had to work but never for himself. To bear up when the Spirit of Truth does not forgive him, he had to aim at the truth all of his life. To satisfy the Spirit of Love he was supposed to do what she wanted. He was unable to and will have to dance to her tune when the time comes.

You receive for the Spirit of Love third of your soul by giving. You receive for the Holy Ghost third of your soul by forgiving. And you receive for the Spirit of Truth third of your soul by understanding how and why the situations, feelings, and knowledge make the Lord's house work in the way it does. This can be learned by going to a performance that will be discussed in the next chapter.

Any way that makes eternity better is good, and anything that makes feelings stronger will help to do it. Three ways of doing it include ideals, decisions, and commitments. A person who sets up ideals very easily will have noticeably stronger feelings as a result. The reason is that a stronger comparison is made between his Heart of Man, where ideals are held, and the knowledge involved. Strong decisions can have a big influence from the Spirit of Truth third of your soul, and promises from the Spirit of Love third.

When you are influenced by an ideal, decision or promise from out of the past, it is called a hang-up. The strongest hang-ups are caused by the decisions. Hang-ups caused by ideals will merely cause the same kind of compulsion feeling as a lifetime habit. Seeing how you created your early-age hang-ups would be very revealing, if you could do it. Even then it would only be the surface manifestation of some spiritual mechanics.

If you will explore your own mind, you will have a much more exciting trip than through any jungle. But the power must come from the Spirit of Truth, not from drugs.

11

The Meaning of Words

Considering that another name for God is life, and that everyone has life, there should be a more direct way of our finding the truth. In the Holy Ghost third of your soul, it is possible to talk with God before the spirit of this world intrudes, usually at a very early age. The spirit of this world, which is pride and death, is a very effective wall. Other feelings and instincts help to form a resistance against getting through to God.

When you try to move in the direction of the Spirit of Truth, the world gets in the way, for Emmanuel has already been "lifted up." And in the direction of the Spirit of Love there stands a wall that everyone will eventually overcome, but this is too far in the future. The material of this wall includes any immoral feeling that has ever been felt in relation to the Spirit of Love. This formidable wall will be useful for eternity, as well as for keeping things hidden in the present.

Eventually, all will reach a high enough level in their marital relations to cross over the top of this wall. This will be a completely new experience, revealing many spiritual insights.

It may seem possible to like a baby well enough, or in some other way to love high enough to cross over this wall, but in the plans of the universe when the first one to make it was asked how he did it, he pointed to the way that carried him over and said, "My carriage."

I remember lifting my Heart of Man out of the way enough to explain that English was the only language used in the beginning, before the world was made. So, the old principle of something being made out of itself was used in forming the English language. English will eventually be the universal language, and no other language will thereafter be in use. All English words have a meaning derived from a combination of words. The word *marriage,* for example, means my carriage.

The male side of this universe was finished before the female side, and both were built by degrees. When a certain member of the Elect decided to see how his wife was progressing, she anticipated trouble and turned to see who was coming. If feelings could be heard, hers would sound like a growl. As she was young and had very curly hair, he went back and told God that she was nothing but a "growl and a curl." The word *girl* is formed from these two sounds.

When this universe had been planned many times over, this same girl was finished. She went to a high level where she could see everything for eternity and looked at her husband's personality. God told her to say how her husband seemed, as fast as she could observe anything about him. His age was then ten years old and full of noise. She started to make a sound like bang or boom, in imitation of a sound she heard, but the rest was all joy. What she said was "boy."

This same fellow ascended to where he also could see everything for eternity, so he could see how she was going to seem to him. He, too, was to say what he saw as fast as he saw it. He started to utter "wonderful," but there was so much life mixed up in it he said "wife."

Words are pronounced differently in some times and places, but they were still made up of other words. A few other examples are: world (we are old); man (my hand) (when God says it); brain (bring pain); husband (house band); evil (Eve will); God (got load); weird (we are God). Although man was created first, he is not at the top yet. Someone should woo man (woman) up higher.

Before the world began, words had meaning for the Spirit of Truth third of a soul, because the words were to have meaning in the future. Words had meaning for the Spirit of Love because of a certain relation with God. Words had meaning for the Holy Ghost because of a phonetic relationship to other words.

Many spiritual things would seem foolish unless the reason

for them was sufficiently understood. There are spiritual truths that can't be told without sounding like fairy tales, for the reason that there are nursery rhymes and stories written for children that have spiritual truths as a basis. The reason is, so children will have the right kind of feelings. The reality of heaven is made from the feeling of very young children. Most babes can know that something is the truth, because they found out about it before they were born.

One of the Elect is Santa Claus. This is a gift-giving feeling common around Christmas. Besides the original Santa Claus, it is desirable for each person to be able to qualify for this position. All those who try are going to have to pass a test. In this test they will find themselves in the position of a government employee who has the ability to get an unjust law passed that would pay himself an old-age pension. While this might seem honest without too close a look, such action is crooked. The name Santa Claus derives from the sentence, "Say no to crooked laws." There is only so much quantity possible to the spirit of giving; it is possible to use it all on yourself!

Many words are formed by saying a whole sentence so fast that only the high spots are hit, as in *Santa Claus* and *beauty*. The word *beauty* is from the sentence "Bend you to me?"

There is an etymological history of how English words came into being on this world, like the Dutch pronouncing *Saint Nicholas* in a way that sounded like *Santa Claus*. But there are no accidents in this world, as far as God is concerned.

The spiritual history (His story) of this world will be known in the future by anyone who wants to know it. This will be had by going to a spiritual theatre where you watch the people on the screen and presently finding that you have become one of them. The program will be made from what has happened in this world and is being run over again exactly as before. After a while, you will land back in your seat and be watching and listening to the character you have just been. In this way you can become first one, then another, and learn how it is for other people. But it will take many long features just to show some of the main doings of the Elect. This show will be held in the second heaven. Much can be learned this way that would be hard to learn by any other means.

Probably the most fundamental idea in this book is the one explaining all feelings as being knowledge compared to other knowledge, for this explains the reason for all the trouble the world has had and will have, the principle behind pleasure and happiness.

Certain forms of pleasure are comparable to certain specific forms of pain; there is a thin wall between. If there had never been any pain on one side, there could be no pleasure on the other.

If you were feeling a mild form of sensual pleasure and could suddenly have this pleasure compared to a large amount of pain and misery—with the comparison made in such a way that you were not aware of the pain and misery but only of the comparison—then the pleasure which had been mild before would suddenly become very intense.

There is a way that this comparison between the two sides can be made from the pain side of the wall. This is an extreme form of masochism. There is also the sadism of inflicting pain on others, as in the case of a sea captain of ancient times who liked to give a member of his crew a beating, because giving the beating gave the captain strong sexual feelings.

No matter what the perversity, as well as in an ideal marriage, the principle is the same: pleasure is relative to pain. However, the pain that makes you feel pleasure is not the pain you have felt, even though you may have contributed to the grand total. In this case it is your ancestors who are responsible.

In another case, everyone on the same team contributes to it. People in this world are not as self-contained as they seem. Although the principle of comparing good things with the bad remains the same, there are feelings other than pain used for a comparison. When a boy wants a bicycle, he is cultivating a feeling located in the same field used by the rest of the people on his team. Instead of a desire for material things, there is a similar situation involving human relations. One is a desire for friendship. In the first field, the spiritual appearance of the feelings looks like growing corn, and so they have always been called *corn* by the ones who have had to talk about them in the planning of this world.

When you want something, you are growing corn, and when you get it, you are eating it. If it can be grown now and used during the age of the new heaven and new earth, what will be eaten will be only an image of the original made of a different stuff. Everyone then can be born with a complete cornfield that will provide enjoyment for one lifetime. Each time one is reborn he will have a new one. However, if there get to be too many "sheep in the meadow and cows in the corn," something will have to be done about it.

A fundamental change is due in the near future.

When the creation of man is completed, he will be in the image of God. Man's image from the time Lucifer made a devil of himself until the second coming of Christ is to be personified by a being who was created by the first saint. This being was made of nothing permanent, but he was given the same smartness as the one who made him, which is next to Emmanuel. This one's name is Charlemagne.* When he died, he went back where he was before he was created. But when he comes again, it will be with spiritual powers as in 2 Thessalonians 2:9: "Even him, whose coming is after the working of Satan with all power and signs and lying wonders."

There are useful reasons for trouble and evil in this world, and several persons have special jobs that help cause it. For instance, Merlin's job was to build a wall between God and man; Lucifer's job was to create a resistance to work against; and Charlemagne's job is to bring all evil under one head.

This brings up the question of when the second coming of Christ will be. A few things will have to happen first. One is the episode of the four horsemen.

In the Book of Revelation the white horse is famine, the red

---

*At an early age I pronounced this name Shär' mān when talking about the last place, 666, on the Elect. He lived one lifetime on this world, 742-814.

one is war, the black is fear, and the pale one is death. There is a definite feeling to dying, especially if one is dying slowly; a definite feeling behind war, hunger, and fear. All of these are personified by members of the Elect.

When enough people feel the same way, it not only creates a spirit that other people can feel, but the member of the Elect who happens to be that particular feeling will then feel it like something coming up underneath him. With enough famine in the world, as well as enough people engaged in war, and with all the fear and feeling of dying, there would then be four feelings strong enough for each to feel like a horse to the one who sat on it.

When is the time of all this? The plans of this world can split like the forks of a road. There will then be two worlds, with everyone doing exactly the same thing in both, until one thing of a spiritual nature happens in one world, a different spiritual happening in the other. Or one world can come to an end and the other continue. God can change the past as well as the future and has done so many times. The only sure answer is that the second coming of Christ is in the *Year of Jubilo.*

As the end of this age approaches, the United States has become an important world power. The Scriptures refer to this country as Manasses. God asked the one who is the confident executive feeling (the same one who made the names "girl" and "wife") what he thought of the United States. After looking at the plans of its destiny, he replied, "It is made of man asses." This age will end in tribulation, but the age of happy times will follow.

If one had never felt happiness, it would be difficult to explain the feeling to that person. Yet there are many varieties of happiness. A closer association with the Spirit of Truth through something even worse than the present Heart of Man will make a wide variety of happiness, and much stronger, as in 1 Cor. 2:9: "But as it is written, Eye hath not seen, nor ear heard, neither have entered into the Heart of Man, the things which God hath prepared for them that love him."

This word *love* is often ambiguous. In some story plots a

married man and another woman plan to murder the man's wife, and the reason given is they are in love. The Bible says everyone should love everyone. But there are two kinds of love. Platonic love is caused by a desire to help someone, which is the usual meaning of it as found in the Bible. Platonic is just another name for the love for which the Spirit of Love is responsible. It is caused by the comparison between your Heart of Man and the knowledge of each and every time any person ever wanted to help another individual, plus a memory of how it felt to your ancestors.

If you make a promise to help someone and faithfully fulfill it, this will tend to make the feeling stronger, because the Spirit of Love third of your mind holds commitments.

Sensual love is love experienced through any one or more of your five senses, the sense of touch being the strongest. While not necessarily coarse, the object of sensual love is to possess the one you love. Add high ideals or platonic love, and you would want to get married. When this desire is connected with ideals so low as to cause a sex crime, the word *love* seems contradictory.

There is a situation called *falling in love,* which is usually both feelings together that have built up unawares against a resistance that keeps them hidden, until they suddenly break through into deep feeling. The resistance may be any kind of ideal or decision you have made against becoming involved with the opposite sex.

Although the sense of touch is the strongest in sensual love, so much importance is put on appearance that the sense of sight is the most important of all, and so the question of "good looks" should be investigated.

12

What Looks Mean

Two girls can be walking down the street together, one with the most beauty, the other the prettiest. The cause of these differences in "looks" can be easily explained. Both are imprints or permanent expressions and have nothing to do with the shape of the features. Their significance has been built up to such importance in this world because they are going to be important for eternity.

The foundation for eternal comparison of appearances is a part of the Lord's House, and this will remain the same for eternity. There will be no need for some to be without perfect looks so that those who have these looks will be appreciated.

Within the Elect of 664 people there are many smaller teams for different purposes. One team creates a beauty shop where the best-looking girl in the world has the right to make any other girl as good-looking as she is. The girls on the beauty shop team have sacrificed every good look. This pays for good looks for eternity.

The reason for having teams is that it is too hard for each one to earn and acquire everything for himself. Others will earn it, then sacrifice it, which is one way to give it to everyone else.

There are a large number of tasks. The most important was what Emmanuel and his disciples did in overcoming death for the rest of the world. Emmanuel had earned the right not to have to go into death, and so doing it was a sacrifice. He now has the right to bring all of those who are in death back to life. Making the knowledge known to the rest of the world was the task of his disciples.

The main one on the beauty shop team is the one with all the good looks. While the other girls of the team sacrificed looks, she planned her life to attain all good looks during this lifetime.

There is an objective and a subjective reason for beauty. For example, suppose two men look at the same painting. One man may think it is very beautiful, while the other may not see anything beautiful about it. The objective reason why it is beautiful lies in the object itself, but the subject of this impression of beauty has to be explained by revealing how a person's mind works. If all minds were the same, the picture would look the same to everybody.

Everything you ever did, said, or thought has left an imprint on your face. Three things determine the force of the imprint. One is how strong was the thought; one is the amount of time you held it; the last is how young you were at the time; the younger you were, the stronger the imprint.

Some girls noticed how they were feeling when they were talking to God before they were born, and as a result told God they loved Him. This is beauty in its spiritual form. If saying it made them feel it stronger, then this accomplished some good; otherwise, it is only the feeling that counts. The stronger the love the stronger the imprint.

The Holy Spirit, which seems like a part of yourself, is not only God, but if you could remember far enough back, you would remember when you used to be God. "Ye are gods" (John 10:34).

So, to explain the beauty of the most beautiful girls, the objective reason for their beauty is because they told God they loved him. That left the imprint on their faces. The subjective reason why we enjoy it is that they were almost talking to us when they said it.

Some girls have tried harder than others to make the sexual side of life better for eternity, when they were planning their lives before they were born. This also left an imprint on each face—a pretty look.

To use familiar faces as examples, a photograph of the face of Loretta Young, as a young woman, will show a very strong beauty imprint. That of Shirley Maclaine will show a pretty look

the strongest. It takes keen perception to see the difference between a beauty imprint and a pretty look; especially on the
same face.

Before a male is born if he likes God it will give him a
good-looking imprint. The ones who tried hard enough to make
the sexual side of life better will have a look that few boys like
who have it; on a girl it would be called pretty.

Because of the mental difference between the sexes, good
looks will show up much plainer to anyone of the opposite sex
than to one's own, for there is as much difference between men
and women mentally as there is physically.

Each member of the Elect has a characteristic look, and if
one continually came up in your mind, you would also acquire
those same looks. Sometimes this look is an overall facial expression, but many times it is a particular type of feature.

In many cases old people will look alike, if they have lived
together most of their lives. This is caused by noticing how each
other thinks and unconsciously imitating it. After sharing the
same kind of feelings for a number of years, they will both resemble the one or more members of the Elect who brought to
their consciousness the knowledge that caused those particular
feelings.

If you saw a stranger who was feeling a high degree of
emotion, such as sorrow, embarrassment, wonderment, guilt,
wistfulness or others, you might know how he felt by his looks.
But since you never saw him before, how do you know he
doesn't look that way all the time? The answer is, each look is
a member of the Elect who looks much the same under any
expression, if you can see through the person well enough.

There is a way to see through people, to see what kind of
character they have, and a way to see their feelings to tell what
they are thinking about; for each thought will express itself,
however slightly, on the features.

The way to tell the character is to notice everything you
can see about the person's looks, including features, permanent
expressions, and imprints, then act as if you looked that way
yourself. While acting, look inside yourself to see what kind of

person you would have to be in order to have looks like that yourself. You inherit some kind of looks, but what you do, feel, and think will change them.

Many people have one or more looks they would not want everyone else to know about, if they knew what caused them, for all looks have a special meaning. What each look means is based on what caused that particular look. Very few looks are inherited, but when one is inherited, it is usually a mental quality which is in turn what caused the physical look. Thus, it may be seen that looks show the character. The average adult has made most of his own looks.

To see through a person, to know what he is thinking about, you should notice every expression on his face, every inflection in his voice, while you are acting as though it is you who looks and sounds that way. Without the acting, you can't tell much. If you are talking to someone and wish to know what he thinks about it while you are talking, then mentally run around and get behind him.

Those who start young enough can acquire the ability to see a screen under anyone's face. This screen is really spiritual, but in this world it resembles a sheet with wrinkles on it, and every thought will change it. These wrinkles are sometimes called pictures by anyone who can see them well.

Anyone who acts as much as he would have to in order to see other people's feelings and character very well, will also change his own looks slightly. He will develop what is called an actor's nose, which has an artistic shape. The profile has nothing to do with it, but John Barrymore had that expression to his nose.

A broad base at the center of a person's nose is called a sharp nose look, and is caused by his turning around and looking back across the first heaven while his body remains unconscious. Many have done this when they were very young, then forgotten it later. Others have kept it a secret because they were told to. Some have used it as a source of information. One person they could see and talk to was Lucifer, but he told them to keep it a secret.

At least seventy-five looks are distinctive enough to describe. Each has a logical reason for being that way. Many are the characteristic looks of certain members of the Elect.

There have been arguments over which are the most intelligent, brows that are high or low. Whether eyebrows are high or low has no connection with intelligence. This difference is caused by two kinds of thinking when very young.

A baby can easily think about things it knew before it was born. If a baby gets in the habit of pondering over these things, it will have deep-set eyes with low brows. High brows are caused by a baby exploring with its eyes, by noticing every new and surprising thing that comes along, anything that will cause feelings. When babies notice their own feelings and puzzle over what they are, their eyebrows tend to grow together in the center. Eyebrows that are wide apart were caused by trying to figure out the things that were looked at.

There can be many combinations, as thinking back about spiritual things and also trying to figure out the things that are seen. This would cause low eyebrows set wide apart. A rare combination would be looking at interesting things of this world enough to make your eyebrows high and also look in at your own feelings enough to make the brows grow together.

Some looks would reveal too much of the personal lives of those who possessed them, if their causes were known. The looks that compliment a person should not be revealed, for that would insult everyone who had the opposite type of look. The origin of looks helps to show the power of thought.

An important question is, What does God think? This entire universe appears to be something that God runs. If you had an imagination that was vivid enough, you could visualize a very complicated machine and run it in your imagination. That would be no more mental than the way this world is run.

13

The World Is Mental

The most advanced knowledge, it seems, would be the knowledge of how God thinks. In the creation, a principle of going around in circles and cycles is frequently encountered. Understanding how these principles work is the main part to the problem of how God thinks.

The way God thinks in a circle is through each of the heavens and back to Himself. The consequences of everything God says is thought of to eternity, which begins when time ends.

Much of this universe was created in parts, then put together like the colors of a picture that are printed separately. This can be done, because it is possible to be in many places at the same time. If you experience one thing at one place, one at another, it can seem as if you are only in the one place, but both the experiences are present simultaneously.

This world from the center outward is traveling through a tunnel which is gradually coming to a vanishing point. Suppose you were walking down a tunnel where your head didn't quite touch the ceiling. If the tunnel not only got smaller so that it came to a point but you got smaller as you went forward, you could go on walking forever without coming to the end. To you the tunnel would be infinitely long; to God it would be finite.

If you were traveling down this tunnel in a car in which the car, the tunnel, and you were all getting smaller, you could not only continue at what appeared to be a constant rate of speed, but you could even accelerate at the rate of thirty-two feet per second every second without reaching the end within any given time.

The center of the world is in the center of the tunnel, and the surface of the world where you are is also in the center of the tunnel. When in a standing position, you are going head first down this tunnel. In this case the world is accelerating at the rate of thirty-two feet per second in its apparent relation to the walls of the tunnel. Gravity not only acts like a constant acceleration, but that is what it is.

The effect of gravity is the same as if God thought for the center of each atom to have an attraction for the center of every other atom. What is hard to see is what method of mental or spiritual mechanics is used to accomplish this, what a stage magician would call the *modus operandi* of the trick.

The world is so much of a mental nature, where everyone who is born across the top of the first heaven carries the whole world around in his head, that it is like traveling through empty space where you put something in front of yourself as you go along. What you see is there because you see it. If you don't go that way with any of your five senses, then you don't need to put anything there. You don't consciously put something in front of yourself, for your mind is made of many parts and these parts do it for you as automatically as a machine would do.

It would be true to say that this is an imaginary universe, that the whole thing is at different levels in God's imagination. The world and everything that can be seen from it are at one level with the first heaven the next highest. Death is a place lower than this world, while hell is the lowest.

The trouble with explaining the universe in such a broad way is that it doesn't explain how God can create it or run it. It is difficult to see how any mind can even keep track of the grains of sand on a single beach.

Actually, God doesn't have to remember where anything is but merely to look at it. The problem to solve is *how* God thinks. Some people might believe this is impossible for anyone to figure out, but whenever there is a question whether something is possible or not, there is a rule. All that is necessary is to know two things: whether you have time to do it, and whether it is actually desirable that it be done.

If you have to do something in a certain length of time, it

may be impossible to finish within that period. And if someone very young tried to pull a pan of hot water off the stove onto his head, it doesn't matter how much desire he has; it still is not desirable. All things considered, if a thing is desirable and time is sufficient, it *has* to be possible. The universe was created so that it would be.

If you are trying to solve a problem, the way to the answer is to study the problem, for the problem and the answer are together. *You can't understand a problem perfectly without knowing the answer.* If thinking is defined as the discovery of a fact, then no time goes by while you think. This is like going by a board fence where the boards represent time. Where there are no boards, there is no time. You look through the cracks to see the answer.

If the problem is how does God keep track of the grains of sand on a beach, then instead of just thinking what sand looks like, you would have to know what a grain of sand really is in order to understand this problem perfectly. If you knew all there was to know about this, you would know how the atoms and molecules worked. With that you would have the answer.

When a jigsaw puzzle is put together perfectly, the proof that a particular piece is a part of the picture is because it fits. Yet before the puzzle is put together, there may be no proof that any piece is a part of the picture, and that is the only proof for some statements in this book, especially on how the universe was created. The statements have to be stated first, then assembled.

One of the most complicated features of creation is the problem of time. In an objective sense, time is relative. For instance, a car goes a certain distance while the earth turns a certain degree. The passing of time in relation to an intelligence, however, can be at almost any rate. The more that is learned about some aspects of it, the more puzzling it becomes.

14

Problems of Time

There are cases of people on the verge of death who have seen in a moment their whole lives before them. Each incident was seen simultaneously, with a suddenly developed faculty for comprehending the whole and each of its parts.

After slipping off the roof of an old mill headfirst when playing, at the age of twelve, I would have landed headfirst but for a piece of the building sticking out, which I could grab. By holding on the right length of time, I would turn backward for half a revolution and land on my feet. In the fraction of a second it took to think when to turn loose, there seemed to be plenty of time for anything. It left in me a strong sensation of brightness.

It is necessary to understand infinity and use it as a stepping-stone, in order to understand time completely. However, there is a principle used both in the heavens and on earth that helps explain how time can be shorter in one place than in another.

Supposing three men plan their lives to be born at the same time, live fifty years, then die at the same time. If one divides his life into fifty pieces and begins living each piece at the same time, he can come down to this world and be back again after an absence of one year, although fifty years went by in his lifetime. Anyone's lifetime is just plans with feelings added.

If the second man divided his life into as many pieces as there were months in his life, he could live his fifty years and be back after an absence of one month. His lifetime would seem just as long to him as that of the first man.

If the third man divided his lifetime into as many pieces as there were days in his life, he could live his fifty years in one day's time. The fifty years would seem as long to him as it did to the other two.

Each of the heavens has its own particular lengths of time, each different from the other and from earth.

It is normal to think of time as something simple, but everything on this world can stand still or be run backwards, including everyone's memory. If the ones in the third heaven want to stop time on this world, they have merely to stop doing the work they normally do. If they run what they are doing backwards, then this world runs backwards. If God runs things backward, then all the heavens run backwards, and none of them know it. They merely find themselves further back in time without knowing they had ever been ahead in time.

There are two main problems with time. One is to keep exerything from happening instantly, and the other is to make time go by at all.

All who are born across the top of the first heaven have their lives divided into small pieces; they begin each of these as if they had already lived their lives up to that time. There is a time and a place where anyone will be able to look back on the life he lived on this world, and it will seem as if it took just three seconds to live it.

If everything can happen at once, and if you are going through your lifetime on this world in only three seconds, then the natural question is, What time is now? Broadly, the answer is: now is the time that you have life.

The way you receive life helps to explain how God is omnipotent. God is omnipotent by traveling from first one to another of all those who are born across the top of the first heaven and who have reached a condition called the age of accountability. Emmanuel did not reach this class until he was baptized, but most reached this stage when they were very young.

Beginning with the youngest of these: that is where the Holy Spirit is and nowhere else. Then He is the next to the youngest one, and after that the next; this continues until He is the oldest human in the world. Each time it is just God without His knowledge; in this form He is called the Holy Spirit. The Holy

Spirit is the ultimate source of all life. The plant kingdom has life only because the spirit behind each plant has life. It is that way for each form of life, but only humans receiving life directly.

This process will eventually end. Eternity will be God as three: the Spirit of Truth, the Spirit of Love, and the Holy Ghost. With no interference from a long line of ancestors, they will have all knowledge of heaven and earth. For the human family to get the most good from this, the other two will have to be lifted up as only Emmanuel has been. This will bring about a condition of the world mentioned in Isaiah Chapter 11: "The wolf shall dwell with the lamb, . . . They shall not hurt nor destroy in all my holy mountain: for the earth shall be full of the knowledge of the Lord, as the waters cover the sea." Everyone today feels only one-third alive compared to the way he will in the future.

All trouble will be past before that age arrives. Otherwise, if you were already unhappy, you would then be three times as unhappy.

It would be more exact to say that happiness is caused by drawing closer to God through the Heart of Man, instead of closer to the Spirit of Truth, but the Spirit of Truth is the only way at this time, so this amounts to the same thing. The lifting up process will be applied to the others when the time comes.

It might be said of God going through the world this way that He lands on first one person, then another. When God enters each human until He is the oldest, there are so many people that He tires, and this can be felt by everyone as he gets older.

If you lived in the days of Abraham when there were not very many people in the world, you might live to be hundreds of years old and still feel young.

Each time that God becomes each of the humans until He is the oldest, He then renews himself through the heavens. He does this by coming down through the sixth, fifth, and fourth heaven, becoming each of the angels in turn, and from there He lands on Lucifer. From Lucifer He goes to those on the world, beginning with the youngest, for everyone has to come by Lucifer before he is born.

After being the youngest, He becomes the next to the youngest, by starting in with the third heaven and coming down through the angels of the first heaven, this time skipping Lucifer. From the angels of the first heaven He goes to the next youngest. Everything that grows is controlled by the angels of the first heaven; from them He gets the next oldest each time until He is again the oldest human being; then He renews Himself down through all the angels of the sixth, fifth, and fourth heavens, from there to Lucifer, where He again becomes the youngest in this class.

In being omnipotent by being first one person and then another, God changes places with the speed of infinity, so that after becoming each person in turn, no time has passed in the world. This creates the problem of how to make time pass at all. This problem began with Adam. To make time pass now, you are traveling on two tracks through this world. Your memory exists for only one side. The other is to make time go by. An explanation of time is likely to be more confusing than clarifying.

Two fellows I knew did opposite things before they were born. One apparently made a wisecrack to God and referred to himself as a dumbbell. The other remarked that he was too smart when he was trying to plan his life to make a certain mistake, and was unable to. The first was never to acquire more than a third-grade education.

The younger you are when you think anything, the stronger an imprint it will leave on you physically. To tell God before you were born that you were a dumbbell will make the blood vessels in your brain grow so small you will not be able to make your brain function very well.

The other fellow could remember what he had seen so well that he thought everyone else had a poor memory. What puzzled him most was that when he remembered anything that was moving, such as an automobile, he could never make it appear moving in his memory, even though he could see every detail. What he was doing was looking through his memories at the actual plans of his life, called a photographic memory.

As you experience the plans of your life through your senses, the plans are compared to your memories and instincts, and the comparison creates a feeling. This feeling is divided into three-second blocks of time.

The way the world looks, sounds, feels, smells, and tastes is made from feelings which at this time in history are mostly an inherited memory of the sensations caused by certain knowledge compared to other knowledge. The sensation of time going by is caused by a definite amount of spiritual thinking that must take place between each three-second block of knowledge. These time bricks feather out to a thin edge and lap over, so it is usually impossible to tell where one leaves off and another begins.

Besides the sensation of time, some spiritual mechanics are involved in making time pass. If someone could read your mind so well that if you had read a book, he could look back in your mind and read it out of your mind, that kind of mind reader could stop at any place in your mind, and it would look like a photograph. If he went along at the same speed as time, he would see things as they looked to you.

However, while he is looking at just one place in your memory, trying to look ahead as slowly as possible, he would see the next frame of time, which would look like the last one. Whatever the speed is at which he can recognize individual pictures, the speed of time is infinitely faster. So, it is necessary to understand infinity in order to understand time.

The basic principle of infinity is that everything must start with God and end with God; otherwise, it is not infinite.

It is desirable that everyone should eventually acquire a knowledge of infinity. A way was invented to help explain it when the time comes. This invention is an ordinary deck of playing cards. No matter what other reasons there were for playing cards, there was a spiritual reason. They can help show how everything has an effect that goes through all of the heavens and returns to its starting place.

The greatst trinity is the body, the soul, and the Holy Spirit—this includes everything, for the body includes all the heavens.

In planning out this universe to eternity, then running it back, and planning it over again and each time, building it up more substantially, there is the problem of how everything can remain in its position. A deck of cards can be used to help explain.

You will need to know how to play a form of solitaire called clock sol. Arrange the cards in piles of four cards each, face down, corresponding to the numerals on a clock with one stack in the center as in Figure 1, A.

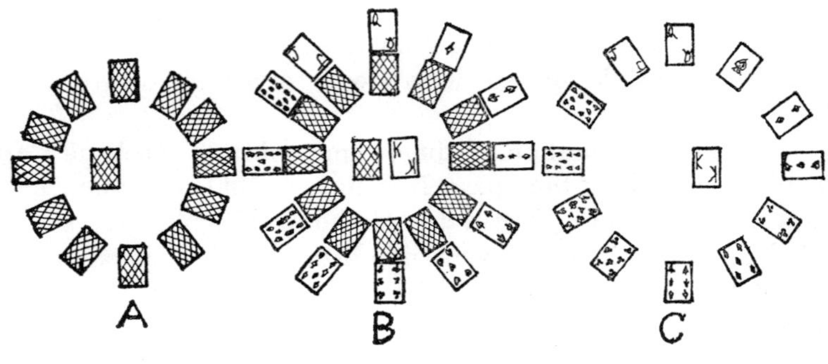

A   B   C

FIG. 1

Begin by turning up a card from the center. If it is an ace, put it by the one o'clock position; if a six, then at the six o'clock position; and each card by its corresponding position on a clock. In each case turn over a card from the new position and place it where it belongs. When the game is partially finished, it will look like *B* in Figure 1, and when it is finished, and if you win, it will look like *C* in Figure 1.

If you now try to play each card backwards so each one goes back where it came from and the cards end up in their original positions, you will find the same kind of difficulty in trying to keep track of everything you would have in running this universe backwards.

A dualism in the universe makes it easy to do so, however. To use the same system in clock solitaire you will need two decks of cards. With one arranged as *A* in Figure 1, and the other as *C* in Figure 1, begin playing *A* in the usual manner, but each time you play a card from this deck then play one in the opposite direction from the deck arranged as in *C.* One deck will be played forwards at the same time the other is played backwards.

To do this in the way the universe was created, you would have to start with only one suit in each deck. Instead of four cards in a pile there would be only one the first time. After playing to the end and back again, add another layer of cards. By using an unlimited number of cards each pile could be built up to any thickness. The universe was planned to the end and back again with another layer of reality added each time, until it was planned an infinite number of times.

The dualism in the universe is the plans of each person's life for one side, and the feelings caused by the same plans as they are compared with each person's Heart of Man for the other side. This latter way represent the world in a more spiritual form. Why one of these equals the other is extremely complicated to explain. The world in its spiritual form can be run backwards from eternity each time the plans are run forward.

To follow the truth in seeing the difference between the way this universe seems and the way it is spiritually, will lead you through evolutions and revolutions. It would be to understand how all of the Elect and the heavens are used to make this world seem real to everyone. But no matter how complicated this world is, it is a creation requiring a creator.

Besides the other things mentioned, the Elect are an integral part in its creation. Each member of the Elect is also a law where each law precedes the next, until they go around in a circle and come back to where they started.

The connection of these two ends is the link between the mental and the physical. To understand the fundamentals of this physical world it is necessary to realize that atoms and molecules can be mental as well as apparently physical.

Knowing what atoms look like, or the answer to any scientific problem is not as important as spiritual knowledge; but there is a close connection.

15

Description of
an Atom

You have perhaps pondered the question of the nature of atoms many times. How do they look? How were they made? How do they behave? Any description of an atom will be more interesting if you have already studied the atomic theories of the past. In one, it looked like a miniature universe; in another, a wave; in still another, a combination wave-and-particle.

At first, atoms were imagined as solid particles that could not be divided into smaller particles. As more chemical and electrical phenomena were discovered which could not be explained, there were many changes in the atomic theory.

The first time I explained what an atom looked like was to another boy who asked about it. I made no attempt to make it explain anything else, but now I see that it fits very well.

If you could barely see a single atom, such as an atom of gold, it would look like a tire in its general shape. If you could see it more distinctly, you would see that the ring of gold was made from other rings. In the case of gold, there would be 79. A closer look would show that these rings were really loops, as in a coil spring. If you took a coil spring with 79 loops and bent it around into a circle and welded the ends together so that no one could tell where the joint was, this would be the shape of a gold atom. An iron atom would have 26 loops, oxygen 8, and each according to its atomic number. An even closer look at these loops would show that they in turn were made of other loops. You would have an infinite number of times to go before you came to a loop that was not made out of another loop.

Since no one enters into an atom, so to speak, these other

130

loops don't exist. To make this universe the way it is takes four generations of loops, including the big one, which is the atom.

Since all atoms are made out of this same kind of loop, and since the hydrogen atom has only one loop in each coil, there has been evidence to cause some scientists to believe that all other atoms were made of hydrogen atoms.

Another way to visualize an atom is to start at the other end and work up to the atom. At this end there is no heat, and so the elements that are normally gases are all solids.

If you want to make an iron atom by starting this way, you will need an iron wire of infinite length and coil this into a spring of infinite length. When you coil this into another spring of infinite length, each loop should contain 26 loops of the previous spring. This should be repeated by making a bigger spring from the same ones you have already made. After you have done this an infinite number of times, you must bend the ends around and fasten them together. Your atom then will be infinitely large.

Actually, the number which is one less than infinity is any number from one to infinity, depending on the step from the finite to the infinite. Making three coils is enough. And another name for infinity is enough. It is one, two, three, infinity.

The atom exists between two infinites; the smallest molecule is infinitely larger than an atom, and an atom is infinitely larger than its own beginning.

The principle of how God thinks to infinity may not be as hard to understand as it seems. For example, if you lived under an arrangement in which you were to receive 25 percent on your money, if you earned $100, you could collect an extra $25 on it. The $25 would be yours, so you could now collect an extra $6.25 on that, then 25 percent of the $6.25. If you kept on collecting, you would have any number of times until infinity in which to collect. But since time is passing while you are collecting, you will never reach infinity that way.

It can be proven mathematically that if you went all the way to infinity and collected an infinite number of times, then added all of your money, you would have $133.33 ⅓. So, infinity can be as definite as any other number. In this universe God thinks to infinity each time he thinks, while man never does. The infinite number of possible times you can collect represents this material universe as it seems to your senses. There is as much of it as you have time to experience.

This world exists in a physical state, which is more apparent than real, but it also exists in a mathematical state, for God is a mathematical God who counts on his ninety-five fingers. This figure is arrived at by dividing the number of the active members of the Elect (665) by the seven heavens, for there were actually 95 elements created in the beginning.

When you think of keeping track of the grains of sand on a beach, you are apt to form a mental picture of the sand; but God has a different way. The way this world looks now is really an illusion.

The reason for the age of the dinosaurs was to help establish this world. A dinosaur saw the world mostly as symbols. If you could be a dinosaur and then come back with a good memory of the experience, you would think that a dinosaur was blind, even though it was not. Each family of these creatures had a spirit behind it, and each of these spirits was a member of the Elect, one object being to let the Elect experience the world.

Suppose you could sit in a chair and push a button that would produce feelings in your legs similar to walking across the floor; have a second button to push that would cause you to hear the sound of a chair squeaking, as though you stood up, followed by the sound of footsteps under you. Supposing also that you would have a stereoscope viewer that would show a wall ten feet in front of you with a door in it. When you looked through the viewer, it would look as if you stood up and walked towards the door.

If you now run all three of these together, the experience would be the same as if you stood up and walked towards the door. If these three could be controlled by your will instead of by buttons, you might walk out through the door and forget that you were in an artificial world. Yet this world you are in now is no less artificial than that one. In this present age the illusion of reality is pretty well established, mostly by the inherited memories from a long line of ancestors, both human and sub-human.

The hearing of sounds is in the same class as seeing illusions. There are four sound ranges or muses. Other spirits connected with singing and speech were called muses by the ancients, but originally there were only four. The four members who make the sounds have the same relative positions they had in producing the illusion of this material world. There is the crystal, corresponding to the low notes; the molecule, the next highest notes; the atom, the next highest notes; and the one who is the beginning of the atom, creating the high frequency sounds without limit.

If an atom could be seen, it would still be an illusion, the same as the rest of the world. But the illusion itself had to be created in some way.

16

Making Atoms

When atoms were originally created, the plans of the universe were already completed from the beginning to eternity. Those who made the atoms looked the same then as they were going to look in the world.

The primary ones were the same four used in other things, such as the making of colors. It would be partly true to say God is in many places at the same time and does different things at different places.

In one of these places the order of this universe had to be decided, and the way it works had to be invented. This is the number six place on the Elect. From this position the rest were told what to do. The one who invents a machine is the best one to run it.

Hypnotism has been used on the stage for entertainment. Some of it is fake, which has led to the idea that all hypnotism is a fake. But the principle behind hypnotism was used in the creation of atoms.

Those of the Elect who did the most in making atoms were the Holy Ghost, the Spirit of Love, the Spirit of Truth, and he who makes the competent and confident executive feelings. By his shorter name he is called Boss. The first three were told to stand in a triangle about ten feet apart and wait. When the Boss came back, he showed the Spirit of Love a card with a drawing on it (Figure 2).

He told her she was to stand at *A* and look down the center of the tunnel as far as she could see. He next told Emmanuel to stand at *B* and look at the Spirit of Love. When he next walked over to the Holy Ghost, he turned the card over without any of them knowing it. On the other side was another drawing (Figure 3).

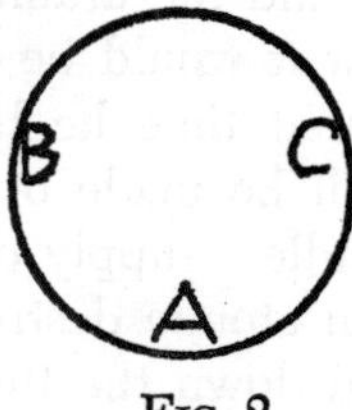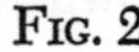

FIG. 2

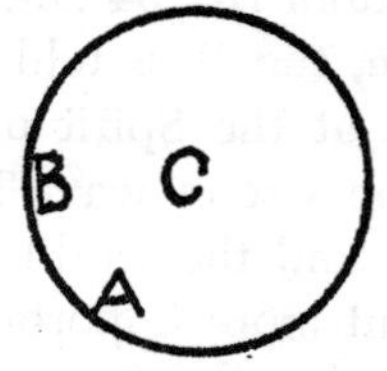

FIG. 3

The Boss told the Holy Ghost to stand at *C* and also look at the Spirit of Love. All of them then walked over to where the tunnel was supposed to be.

When one is hypnotized and told there is a Christmas tree standing in the corner full of decorations, he can be made to see it as vividly as if it were there. Whether the tunnel was there before it was created doesn't matter as long as they saw it. Actually, the foundation was already in their minds, for the universe was completely planned before atoms were made.

When the Spirit of Love looked down the tunnel, the walls of the tunnel seemed to converge in the distance. The walls were straight, but this illusionary point makes possible an infinite smallness.

Where the Spirit of Truth was standing, a row of positions ran down the tunnel like a path. Each position was for a member of the Elect. The Spirit of Truth was told to stand on every seventh position.

In the process of making atoms, something could be seen flowing through the tunnel, as if the atmosphere were slightly visible. It would be right to call this "time." It was also traveling at a high rate of speed at the instant it started.

Part of this flow through the tunnel had to travel from the Spirit of Truth to the Spirit of Love, which made a spiral twist as it came down the tunnel. Since Emmanuel was a short distance down the tunnel on the seventh position when they began making the first atom, the loops of the spiral were close together. As soon as enough were made to make atom 95, Emmanuel moved down seven positions. The number of loops required for this first atom was $1 \times 95 \times 95 \times 95$.

After atom No. 94 and 93 were made and the uranium atom was begun, the Boss told the Holy Ghost it would be better if he looked at the Spirit of Love. Until that time he had been looking the wrong way. These atoms will be made over again some day, and the world will have an endless supply of atomic energy; but more important, be safe from atomic destruction.

The farther the Spirit of Truth moved down the tunnel, the slower time flowed. When the last atom was made, which was hydrogen, time was moving very slowly, but only one complete revolution or loop in the spiral was needed; therefore it took no longer to make the last atom. When the helium atom was made, which was next to the last, the number of loops made for it was $1 \times 2 \times 2 \times 2$.

Where the tunnel is imagined as coming to a point and the car, the tunnel, and you are getting small together, it could seem like going on forever at a constant acceleration. However, if an outside observer could see through the wall of the tunnel, he would see that you were slowing down in relation to the atmosphere through which you were traveling.

Everything is relative in this universe. Instead of traveling down a tunnel that comes to a point and continually growing smaller, it would be possible to stand still looking down the tunnel while the atmosphere of the tunnel flows past you at an increasingly slow rate and get the same effect.

The atmosphere of the tunnel, by its continually slowing down, affects the speed of light, so that light traveling through the universe will take longer now than it did in the past.

Astronomers have noticed that very distant stars will consistently give light of a longer wave length, meaning the red end of the spectrum. If this was caused for the same reason that a train whistle drops in pitch as the train goes by, then the stars at a great distance would have to be traveling away at a high speed. This is called the expanding-universe theory. However, all light is traveling slower now than it was millions of years ago, and since it takes millions of years for light to travel from distant stars to the earth, the light that started out at a higher frequency at that time now has a slower frequency, which makes it redder.

While the Holy Ghost and the Spirit of Truth were looking at the Spirit of Love and she was looking at infinity, the Boss could see three surfaces inside the smaller tunnel, which were placed like a triangle (Figure 4). These acted as perfect mirrors.

FIG. 4

It is common to think of the world as being composed of many atoms. Actually, there was only one of each created, and the rest are all live images that perform on a field according to definite laws. If you wish to see what this field looks like, you should take three mirrors of the same length and arrange them as in Figure 4. Looking down this triangle, you will see what looks like a cube made out of wire. Instead of seeing the cube from the side, you are looking at it from one corner with the opposite corner directly behind it.

After time had gone all the way in making atoms, it was run backwards. If time is examined closely, it would be seen as the plans of the universe. If you entered into time at any point, you would have been at that point in history.

After the atom making was finished, the tunnel, which in effect came to a point, was bent into a circle with the point coming to the center of the bigger end. Everything, including light, was bent with it. So, looking down the tunnel it would appear perfectly straight, but to travel to the end you would need all of time to get there.

If a man with a measuring rod tried to measure this tunnel and in reaching the center was halfway to infinity, his measuring rod would be only half as long as when he started. He would never get there. But God thinks to infinity by considering the angle of the walls of the tunnel, which makes the infinite distance very definite. The angle can be determined by the way time is slowing.

Euclidean geometry would say that two parallel lines extending out into space would never come together, and if you could go there and measure them with a ruler, you would think that was right. However, your ruler would then be shorter. The parallel lines do come together in a spiritual sense, though not in a physical one.

There are two kings of the Elect whose job it is to see, one for each eye. First one, then the other looked out from the small end of the tunnel, but the tunnel was curved into a circle, so they were looking into the big end. Everything you see with your eyes is in your own head. Starting at the big end the tunnel leads to a theoretical point, but starting with the small end it gets bigger to infinity. When you look into the big end from the small end, you see just what you see from this world every time you use your eyes, except that now there is an illusion with it.

When I was ten years old, a boy of five would talk about something that puzzled him. He said that besides seeing with his eyes it seemed he could see another way, that what he saw was big and bright and was all over. What he really saw was how the universe looked from the little end of the tunnel, the spiritual side of this physical world.

Space is a created stuff and includes everything material; it had to be figured out like designing a machine. The heavens were also part of the invention. In Heb. 6:20, the words "after the order of Melchisedec" mean this entire universe.

17

Motion of Atoms

Ever since the introduction of the ether theory there have been arguments for and against it. The way radiation travels through space might appropriately be called ether. In that case there are four ethers involved in radio, magnetism, heat, and light. This indicates it would be possible to broadcast power by wireless, although not necessarily desirable.

The principle of broadcasting power is to charge one ether positive and another negative; the receiving end would try to even up the charge. It could be easier to generate power on the spot with an atomic battery or other similar means.

Light travels through the ether that is furnished by the third heaven. Radiant heat, like heat from the sun, travels through a different ether, the one from the sixth heaven. The ether of radio is from the fourth heaven, and magnetism from the first. The fifth heaven deals with electricity traveling through a conductor. The second and seventh heavens are involved in the problem of time.

The problem of time has many ramifications. There is a division in the second heaven, and on one side there is a place that the Bible calls the *Lake of Fire*. This place is important in the meaning of time.

If some people are not going to live forever, then everything that identifies each one as an individual—that is, his entire personality—will be thrown into this place like a bunch of old clothes. There will be no pain in this. After losing all possessions and positions, there is no difference between souls. They will then go back to where they were before they were created and be forgotten. The Lake of Fire acts as the tailhold for time.

From the seventh heaven it would be possible to look on

this world at any point in history, then into the future, and skip around in any direction.

Time is the rate at which things happen. The Lake of Fire goes on for all time but nothing happens, and in the seventh heaven everything happens now. Every other place is in-between.

If you could go to the third heaven and talk to someone there for one minute, then return with no time lost either in going or coming, about one month would still pass during your absence. Time in the fourth heaven is much shorter than in the third. The fifth heaven is even shorter, and in the sixth heaven it has only been a few hours since Emmanuel was living on this world. The times in these heavens are meshed like the gears in a clock.

In the tunnel where atoms were made, the atmosphere was not just the plans of the world but included the plans of the heavens also. Although they were traveling at different speeds, they were all slowing up together. At the place where atoms were made, it was at the same point in history for each of them. These times are also the ethers.

The way these ethers affect the atom is something like a cake of butter with a coil spring in it. If the spring is straight and sticking out the side of the butter, you can remove it without moving the butter by twisting the spring around. But an atom is shaped like a coil spring bent into a perfect circle. If a spring of this shape was in a cake of butter and it was made to rotate, it would also have to twist within itself. If it had ten loops, it would have to twist ten times for each complete revolution. The first heaven's ether acts like the cake of butter to the atom itself in that the atom cannot move in any direction through it. Each of the other ethers act as if it were solid only to its own generation of loops in the atom.

While these ethers act as if they were all in the same place, they are all separate. When you look through a stereoscope, each eye seeing a separate picture, the two pictures appear to be one. This world may appear to be one, but actually its several parts are experienced separately, then superimposed to appear as one.

While there is only one of each of the atoms and the rest

are all reflections, these reflections will be spoken of as if they were atoms since they act the same. They could more accurately be called positions in a created space ready to act like atoms.

It is common to think of a weight that is moving through the air, such as a bullet, as composed of atoms and all of them moving along together. In reality, the atoms in the back of the bullet do a disappearing act only to reappear in the next positions ahead; this happens with all the atoms in the bullet.

There are many empty positions between the atoms, so the back layers of atoms will start moving first. After they all accelerate, they will move along together. The ones in front will disappear, only to reappear in front of where the bullet used to be, and the bullet will then be there. When they come to a position occupied by an oxygen or nitrogen atom, these atoms will disappear and new ones will appear just ahead. This will happen fast enough so that air will be compressed in front of the bullet. When air tries to get out of the way, the same principle applies: atoms disappear and reappear going off to the side.

The bullet, as well as everything else in the world, acts as if it were in more than one place at the same time. In the ether of the third heaven the bullet apparently moves, and this makes it appear to move in this world. In the other ethers it stands still, so that whichever way the atoms are lined up, they try to remain that way. This is important to the four basic forces that exist in nature. They are magnetic force, gravity, the strong nuclear force, and the weak nuclear force.

Molecules travel, because in a special way time and space become synonymous. They travel as long as time is passing. The making of atoms was also the making of space. To say that the plans of the universe were used to make atoms, is to say time was used to make space. The flowing by of the plans is the passing of time. Space is made of time.

Another name for a molecule is a rule for the behavior of the atom. They are the same but for being at different ends of a tunnel. The simplest molecule for each element looks exactly like the atom for that element, except there is an infinity of difference in their size. And the molecules travel. But the effect is the same as if the atom were in the exact center of the molecule, a wheel within a wheel.

In some atomic theories the atom was pictured as a cube, which explained many chemical puzzles, but this cubical behavior of atoms is caused partly by the fixed positions.

Imagine that there are large signboards with a multitude of small lights close together, some lights on, the rest off. The lights that are on can be in the shape of some object. They can form a moving picture by having the lights go out in the back part at the same time more lights go on in front. The picture thus appears to move across the signboard.

This same principle was used three-dimensionally in the creation of this universe which divides space into cubes. Instead of a light being in each position, it is occupied by a complicated phenomenon. If this was all of the world a person could experience, then the world would appear as symbols, for these symbols do nothing but show the position and movement of a spiritual phenomenon that proves, when interpreted rightly, to be material objects. The world looks real to animals, because it looks real to the spirits behind the animals.

The method used in placing these positions and keeping track of them results in a steady tone that everyone hears twenty-four hours a day all his life. But one would have to be stone-deaf to notice it. This tone is made from three tones. One will change if you travel north or south, one east or west, and the other if you go up or down. Some fish and birds use this as a means of finding their way back over thousands of miles. It is the spirit behind each family that does the guiding.

In addition to the tunnel, which is the altitude tunnel used by the Spirit of Love, there were also tunnels made for the others. Any point an atom can be in the universe can be described as a certain distance down these tunnels. This is like having three universes, each one of only one dimension. Instead of looking at these in three states of consciousness, you are able to synchronize them into one state of consciousness. You then have one three-dimensional universe.

The one-dimensional universes do not have to be literally

one-dimensional but can be in the form of long narrow tubes in which something can happen at each place intercepted by the other two. There is also a tunnel for keeping track of time, and so there are four working together as a unit.

When you push against a lead weight hanging from the ceiling by a string, it will move, but its resistance is caused by atoms being forced to speed up. The number of loops in the coil of a lead atom is 82, the first or biggest coil forming the atom itself. But each of the loops in this coil is normally (excepting isotopes) made from 82 more, and they from 82 more. One revolution of the lead atom means the first coil must twist around 82 times, but each loop of that coil must twist 82 times that many times, and each loop of its coil 82 times that many times, or $82 \times 82 \times 82$. So, it takes energy to get it started, and since there is no friction in atoms, it takes just as much to stop it. If you pushed on an aluminum weight, that would be $13 \times 13 \times 13$. That is the reason for the difference in weight between aluminum and lead.

There is a job in the first heaven that looks as if an angel is turning something around on a table. This results in all atoms spinning. To him they are spinning at a constant rate, but in the tunnel where atoms were made time is continually slowing, which is just as if the atoms were speeding up. The only way they can keep from speeding up is to travel along with time down this tunnel towards the center of the earth, falling at the increasing rate of around thitry-two feet per second.

Regarding gravity, the world started with slow-spinning atoms in the dawn of creation, and they have been speeding up ever since. Very little increase in speed is needed each day for everything to maintain its proper weight. When a weight is falling freely, the atoms of the weight are not speeding up.

If you attempted to travel backward through time to the beginning of the universe, you would need all time in which to do it. The way time can travel infinitely fast in relation to the speed of the atom is for the atom to stand still.

When the universe began, there was exactly the same number of each type of atom. This is something like making 95 monuments, one of 95 bricks, one of 94 bricks, and decreasing until the simplest is just one brick. Any rearrangements could result in leftover monuments made of just one brick. When galaxies collide, the effect could be like a wreck of the monuments. There may then be more hydrogen atoms, but in the beginning there were the same number of each. All were standing still in a space that curved in a circle to a point. To any human mind placed in it, this would be an infinite number of atoms in an infinitely large space.

The name of number seven position on the Elect is the Chief Mechanic, and when the universe was standing still, he looked down the tunnel where the Holy Ghost was in the center. In this tunnel the Boss saw four mirrors (Figure 5).

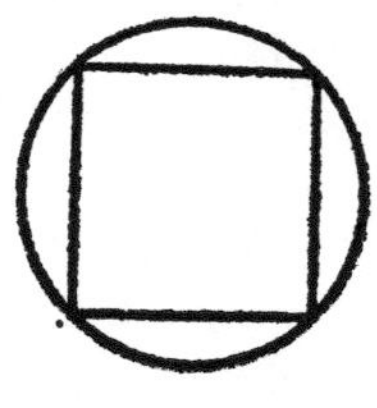

FIG. 5

The object of this arrangement is for molecular motion. When all was ready and the Chief Mechanic was looking down this tunnel, all the heavens began working at the same time. This resulted in the four winds of heaven (the ethers) starting out so fast that nothing like it has ever happened since. The universe then began forming in droplets, the drops coming together to form larger ones with greater distances in-between. Today these drops are called galaxies. Most galaxies are spinning.

Water running out the bottom of a tub will very easily begin whirling around. When a layer of hot air close to the ground held down by a layer of cold air breaks through the cold air, the air coming in from the sides will begin whirling around as it starts up, as in a tornado. Also, stars falling into a common center will begin circling around the center, according to natural laws.

A galaxy may look like a pinwheel spinning so fast that it is flying apart, but it is actually falling together. The spin of most of them is sufficient to keep them from actually collapsing.

The length of time this procedure required was of no consequence, for there could be any amount without any form of life having to wait. There are places where the human race seems very young, but on this planet we are old.

That was the way the physical side of the universe was planned, but to make it look that way to humans who were going to live on earth, all kinds of trickery had to be used in the third heaven.

These chapters are not to make you feel that you understand creation, but to start you off in the right direction in thinking about it. Investigating and comparing other theories can increase your interest in the subject. The atomic theory proposed by Carl F. Krafft of Annandale, Virginia, in his treatise (*The Structure of the Atom*) has much in common with the atom as pictured here. Creative thinking can be very enjoyable.

18

Behavior of Atoms

Because so much is said in this book about atoms, it seems appropriate to show some of the ways in which the atomic theory here presented fits in with some of the riddles in this universe, such as radiation, positive and negative electricity, et cetera.

If you try to explain the riddles of the universe from a materialistic viewpoint, it becomes obvious that atoms are so small in relation to their distances apart, that the necessary weights and inertia loads, when Newton's laws are considered, make a physical explanation of the universe impossible. We need a much broader view.

Since the world was created for the beings who inhabit it, it is necessary to understand the beings to understand its creation. Instead of the material universe being one thing and the life on it something else, they are an inherent part of each other. Whether man is the result of a single cell going through a process of evolution during eons of time, or whether man is the result of divine creation, *these processes are identical!* Life cannot come from non-life, but that was not necessary in putting life on this world, for the basic reality of all material things is life.

All creation is the result of a few fundamentals that have been multiplied and combined with endless variety. When experienced through the senses they become this physical universe. The mental side of you is the fundamentals.

True enough, the Bible states that man was made from the dust of the earth; and since the earth is atoms made of the Elect and the Elect are people, then the world came from people and the people came from the world. This universe is made of itself!

Something as unintelligent as a housefly has a compound eye which is hundreds of individual eyes. One way to see how this world can appear real is to imagine you have billions of eyes, each looking at something very small, such as molecules. Your looking at them establishes them as something that exists. If a part of your life continues to look at individual molecules, while you go around in a circle and look at them from a great distance, so that you can see them as a whole, you then see they look the same as this world looks to you now.

An atom can be infinitely small by being in a certain place, while the effect of the atom is in another. It might be any size where it was made, but where its effect is—which is in the center of the molecule—it is infinitely small.

What is usually called a molecule is the effect of a large number of molecules. What is usually called an atom is here called a molecule. What is usually called the nucleus of an atom is here called the atom. And what is customarily called electrons or other parts of atoms, is here called rings or loops of atoms.

Imagine a molecule at the wide end of a tunnel which then comes to a gradual point at the other end. Imagine an atom at the point of the tunnel with the tunnel curving around into a circle with the atom in the center of the molecule as in Figure 6.

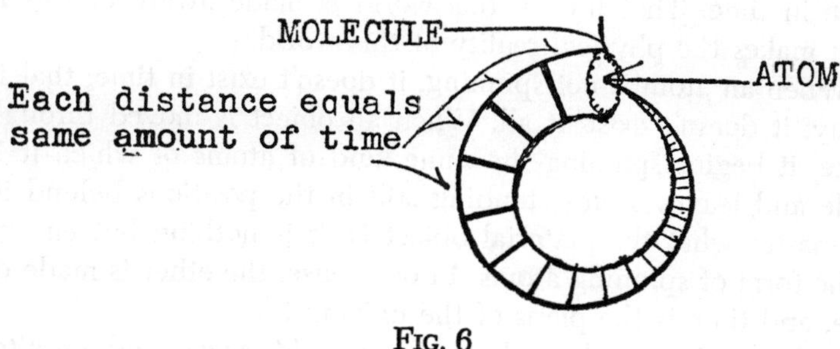

FIG. 6

One atomic theory describes an atom as an outer ring of electrons with a nucleus in the center where its mass is concentrated. This theory resembles the atom and molecule combination described here.

The gravitational field of an atom goes around the universe

and back to itself. As it starts out, it is called radiation; as it comes back, it is called a gravitational field, one which tries to bring all other atoms of the universe in with it. Stars that are enormously heavy for their size are also enormously hot, and high temperature means high frequency radiation.

The reason why a gravitational field tries to gather in all other atoms of the universe is the same reason why a constant acceleration in a car will push you with a steady force against the back of the seat. The reason why a complete revolution at a constant speed represents an acceleration is that time is relative. For example, if you travel down this tunnel for a distance equal to its diameter, this distance represents a definite amount of time, as in Figure 6.

If time were headed towards the small end, there would be an infinite amount of it for anyone who was living in that time. Instead, this universe began with the small end, and you would have to go back through an infinite amount of time to reach the beginning. When time ends, it will be turned around and be when eternity begins.

Each point in space also exists in the form of four numbers. These represent its latitude, longitude, altitude, and a certain place in time. That life on this world is made aware of this is what makes the physical reality of this world.

When an atom is not spinning, it doesn't exist in time; that is to say, it doesn't exist at all. When an object is moved through space, it begins spinning the same kind of atoms of which it is made and leaves atoms standing still in the positions behind it. No matter what the material object is, it is nothing but energy in the form of spinning atoms. In one sense, the ether is made of time, and time is the plans of the universe.

Before going further, the terms *weight, mass,* and *gravitational field* should be defined. Weight is how much anything would weigh in this world. The same object weighed with a spring scale would be less on the moon, more on a heavier planet. The mass of the object would stay the same whether on the moon or the earth and can be described as its resistance to any change in its position or motion.

The word *inertia* could be used in describing mass—the greater the mass, the greater the inertia. The gravitational field of an object is what it contributes to its own weight independent of the gravitational field of the earth. This is analogous to a magnetic field where two magnets attract each other. If either lost its magnetic field, the other would continue its own attraction.

The spin of an atom and the length of the plans of which it is made determine both its mass and gravitational field.

Each kind of atom has its own rate at which time is passing, and this rate does not get out of step with the rest, although various factors try to influence it. When something tries to change it, something of equivalent value will happen. The easiest way to attempt to influence this rate is with heat, for a small amount of time in the sixth heaven is equal to a large amount of time in this world.

If heat were allowed to increase the weight of an atom, there would be big changes in weight with normal changes in temperature. So, when a source of heat tries to speed up an atom, something drastic has to happen.

To understand this more easily, imagine a weight such as an anvil that is heated until it would be fifty percent heavier—if heat were allowed to have that effect. If the anvil becomes heavier, it then has more inertia. Weight and inertia have equivalent values.

Suppose the anvil has a mind of its own and has the choice of accepting the extra weight, which it refuses, or accepting something of equivalent value, which it prefers. If the anvil weighs 50 pounds and the increased weight would have been 25 more, then with the anvil sitting on a frictionless surface with 25 pounds pushing first on one side, until it moved as far or as fast as it wished, then 25 pounds on the other, alternating back and forth, this would equal in value for as long as it was kept up an increase of 25 pounds pushing straight down, which is weight.

When heat tries to increase the speed of an atom, as the atom tries to speed up its molecule speeds up along with it. The molecule begins to travel faster back and forth. This means overcoming inertia as in accelerating any weight. Heat and mechanical energy are interchangeable. This explains the kinetic theory of heat.

When an atom tries to speed up, something else always happens, instead. In the example of the speeding bullet where atoms stop spinning, only to have others begin spinning just ahead in the bullet's path, the atoms are revolving faster while they are there, but a certain amount of time is lost between each jump from one atom to the next. The time lost equals the time gained, and so the total number of revolutions will remain the same.

The weight of an atom is tied directly to its speed, because the atom was created out of time. To increase the speed of rotation of an atom is to increase the rate at which time is passing. If you took an atom apart as it was assembled and laid it out in a straight line, each end of the line would be seen as a point in history. The inertia of an object in space is really inertia of the planned order of that same object in time. Each atom has its own rate of behavior in time. Time can be used instead of space because of the way atoms are connected with life. When life relative to time is seen in a certain roundabout way, it becomes objects in space.

Since the atom and molecule have only to speed up their rotation very slightly to increase the linear acceleration of the molecule, there is a very slight increase of weight with a normal increase in energy. If time had no end, then even a light weight would equal an infinite amount of energy.

Gas molecules will in effect continually hit each other and the walls of their container, so this will offer a way to use any extra energy they receive. Think of a solid placed in a vacuum and heated, as in a radio tube. The molecules would try to behave the same, but those on the surface would have unequal forces pushing one way more than another. Their movement would not be sufficient to give the atoms enough to do in overcoming inertia. When a molecule does not increase its velocity, no additional inertia is being overcome.

When energy is added from a battery, the atoms will either become heavier or do something of equal value. If in this case energy cannot be used up overcoming inertia, what is left is to throw off rings appearing as radiation. The smallest loops of an atom have some length, which in the outside or largest ring would be weight. If the atom deducts the weight as fast as it takes it on, it maintains its equilibrium. Taking on or giving off weight is not as haphazard as it sounds, but usually it is the equivalent of weight that is gained or lost. The atom itself remains the same.

When an atom takes on a certain quantity of electric energy, that is a definite number of rings or loops, and if it cannot use it for overcoming inertia, it gives back an exact amount of radiation. The ratio between the largest coil, which makes the atom itself, and all the coils together, is the ratio between the atomic number and the atomic weight.

Every force that acts on any weight is a push; there are no pulls. If you hook on to something and pull it, the hook reaches around behind and pushes it. Each link in a chain goes behind the next link and pushes. The molecules in a cable have a binding force caused by a field that goes in a circle and pushes on other molecules from behind. If they get too close, another force pushes from in front. Gravitation and magnetism act the same way, with their fields going in a circle and pushing like an acceleration, which they are.

The rotational speed of the atom is not great, but it represents a long period of time divided into three-second blocks of time. These can leave the atom so fast they give the effect of high speed.

The reason why removing a part of the atom slows it down is that if you start at any place on the atom and keep going, you will come back to where you started. When you must travel between two points in a given length of time, in order to slow down your speed you must shorten the distance between the two points. This distance is measured in events. It is the effect given that is important; the effect of spiritual things is what is called reality.

To make this universe work as it does, there has to be something very much faster than the speed of light. The speed of light is the fastest any particle of radiation can travel. Considering how the parts of this universe are coordinated and synchronized, there are large numbers of events in which each must happen before the next and in consecutive order. This is done with the speed of infinity. The speed of infinity is used in locating each point in space where an atom can be. When things happen with the speed of infinity, a large number of things can happen, each before the next with no time between the first and the last.

To understand the way time is involved in the creation of a material universe is very difficult. The first article I read about relativity was in the August, 1929, issue of *Popular Science Monthly,* where it stated: "Einstein brought space to life by enriching it with the 'fourth dimension' of time." In this same article Einstein was quoted as saying: "All four 'dimensions' are so closely interwoven that they depend upon each other. Live vibrating space plays a part in every electric or mechanical action."

No attempt will be made here to interpret anyone else's ideas on the subject, for there are two opposite ways of thinking; one is by analysis, the other by synthesis. To understand creation by analysis means to dissect it. Mathematics would then be an important tool. My own theories were reached by synthesis.

If you propose a set of spiritual principles that will produce an imaginary world with the same appearance as this one, the chances are this one has a similar set of principles. In trying to see through this world and its creation, the meaning of the word *time* needs more explaining than any other part of creation.

Time, space, and the difference between positive and negative electricity have both an objective and a subjective explanation. In the objective, time is determined entirely by events in relation to other events. The subjective is its effect on human minds. Thus, time is half objective, half subjective.

Space in relation to material things is just a place for objects to be. In the creation of this universe, however, space is as complicated as if it were solid, the objects being hollowed-out places inside. One explanation fits both.

The external or objective explanation for the difference between positive and negative electricity is that while both are made of the plans of this universe, one is plans of the future, the other of the past, which makes them try to come together in the present. This also concerns the subjectiveness of time. Every human stands still in time while the plans change both for the future and the past, and the present jumps by in three-second time bricks. They overlap and so are undetected.

The subjective difference between positive and negative electricity has its main principle in the fact that at a certain critical time and place half of the people thought they were equal to God, half thought they were not.

This subject branches out endlessly. For example, each one went to a certain place to see if he was or was not equal with God in this physical universe. Each could see that in going back into time he had all of time; in going out into space he had all of space in which to go. In this way he was equal to God. Since you may not be able to go either out into space or back in time, the answer is that in some ways you are partly equal to God; in no way are you completely equal.

All who went to see if they were equal to God saw that they were; and all who went to see if they were not equal saw they were not—all except number nine position, the handyman. He went to see which way it was and saw that it could be either.

To explain this universe you would not only have to outline the spiritual mechanics involved but also why these spiritual mechanics appear as this universe to the humans who are in it.

The universe is not only of a mental nature, but is centered in each person who was born across the top of the first heaven. It would be more true to say that when you walk along a street, you remain in the same place and the street goes by underneath you; in the passing of time you stand still while your plans go by.

The plans of the universe, including those of everyone's life, are an integral part of its physical creation. When the universe was replanned many times, both the physical and mental side of life became more real, until at last the feelings were as good for eternity as anyone would want them to be. The next time, life was added to the plans and they were run over again, up to the present time.

In trying to grasp the problem of the subjectiveness of time, including how time can seem long at one place and short someplace else, there is evidence to show that where time seems long, it is spiritual trickery. But is that not good enough? If you are looking at a mountain in front of you, it only seems to be there. It really doesn't exist except in your mind, but that also is good enough. Where you go with your five or more senses, that is where the world and the rest of the universe are, "for the spirit of the living creature was in the wheels" (Ezek. 1:20).

One who saw how the atom worked and tried to describe it was Ezekiel in the first chapter of the book of Ezekiel. The atoms do their changing in a straight line in three possible directions and are synchronized with time so that all four remain in step.

The problem of how to have control of so many points in space seems huge, but a good way to have control is to be there. A person could have a soul made of the Holy Spirit and nothing else. In that case he would be an image of a human being. All images seen in the tunnels were thus made, for God provided the mirrors. A member of the Elect would see what looked like his reflection going back and forth to infinity. Instead, each image was able to perform independently of the rest. Everything that exists is made out of life, and the job of unifying everything, including all the heavens, is one that God directs. Also, God determines everything that would otherwise be an accident. So, there is only one chance in infinity of two snowflakes looking exactly alike.

The reason it has been so difficult for scientists to think of an atomic theory that fits all of the observed facts is a principle often used by magicians in performing their tricks.

Many tricks can be done in more than one way. For example, the magician strings an iron washer on a cord, then gives you the ends of the cord to hold and proceeds to take it off without breaking or cutting the cord. He then wonders if he can do this with a paper washer. He does. Each time he holds a handkerchief over it so you cannot see what he does.

If you try to discover one explanation that will fit both, it will be impossible. Trying to figure out atomic behavior is similarly baffling.

It is like having more than one world but having them synchronized, with one world providing one kind of phenomenon, and another providing a second kind; it only seems like one world. There is also the question of how the sun, moon, and stars fit into the picture.

There have been scientific experiments in which the object was to detect the earth's travel through the ether as it orbits the sun. The reasoning is that in going against the source of light, the light should seem faster; in going with the source of light, it should seem slower. The difference would have been detected if the earth did travel through the ether around the sun.

In the third heaven there are a few dozen different earths, and all of them are this earth. When you look at the sun, you look at it from one earth; when you look at the moon, you look at it from a different earth, and each has something in particular with which it is connected. Where the earth and sun operate together, the angel who runs this does so by running the sun around the earth. In each case the earth does not move in any direction but merely spins around. This spinning of the world should be easily detected near the equator by using the proper apparatus for detecting ether drift, such as used by the Michelson-Gale experiment of 1925 and the Sagnac experiment in France in 1913.

In the early days of astronomy, astronomers claimed that certain constellations were moving, while present-day astronomers say they are stationary. What happened is that certain angels of the third heaven who were running these constellations got tired and left to be born on this world, leaving their constellations to appear as fixed stars. Some of these fixed stars are not as far away as they appear.

The bodies of the angels of the third heaven are made of what might be called ether in this world. When an angel steps into his job, he does so as though the earth were not there, for he can move through it, or it through him, with no resistance.

When light strikes your eye, it is as though small particles left the object and came to you, and they *are* mathematical particles traveling in a wavelike manner.

The more specific an explanation of the universe, the harder it will be for some to believe it. Evidence has been presented by astronomers to indicate that the earth is the center of the universe. Science has been reluctant to believe that this world holds a unique position in the universe, and the general belief is that this world is just another planet in every physical way. However, proof will be found.

The earth is not only in the center of the universe, but it is human beings that make the earth exist at all. Life on any other planet is like weeds growing on an island in the ocean. There are other places to go when you leave here, but they are on a different spiritual level.

19

When You Leave This World

Many decades ago, science discovered that neither energy nor weight could be destroyed. If physical energy cannot be destroyed, it would be unscientific to think that any other kind of energy could be destroyed, and that would include life energy. You are alive now, so when you leave this world, you must go somewhere. But where?

Where any kind of energy goes might depend on what kind of energy it is and where it came from. Emmanuel says, "That which is born of the flesh is flesh; and that which is born of the Spirit is spirit" (John 3:6). Many have had such a strong desire to know whether or not to accept Christianity as fundamentally true that when they became convinced it is true, that belief brings a high degree of happiness. That particular feeling is what many ministers have called being born again. But no one in the world has been completely born again, according to what Emmanuel meant when he said, "Except a man be born again, he cannot see the kingdom of God" (John 3:3). The more you allow the Holy Spirit to control you, the more you are being born of the Spirit.

People are much the same physically compared to differences between their spiritual possessions and positions. Heb. 13:2, says: "Be not forgetful to entertain strangers: for thereby some have entertained angels unawares."

All angels and saints will at some time in their existence live a normal life in this world, and many of them already have, for all angels and saints are normal human beings.

When this world was planned out from beginning to end and

157

then run backwards and planned over again, each time becoming a little more perfect, the first to be ready was the youngest angel in the sixth heaven. All other angels down through the heavens were next, and on to the Holy Ghost position and the rest of the Elect in that order. The next time the universe started forward, everyone began working along with it.

This time when something was ready to grow, it had a spirit behind it. If it was high enough up the evolutionary ladder, it had a soul.

The Holy Ghost, the Spirit of Love, and the Spirit of Truth can be in as many places at the same time as needed. They formed the souls directly for each person who was born across the top of the first heaven. Each lower form of life has a soul formed by the trinity from the spirit behind it. Even a low form of life has a soul, formed in a subdivided way of the Holy Ghost, the Spirit of Love, and the Spirit of Truth. A soul is just a certain connection between these three. The symbol for a soul could be drawn as in Figure 7.

These rings can be taken apart and put together without breaking any one of them, for they are really the ends of three tubes as in Figure 8. Both ends of each tube make one ring.

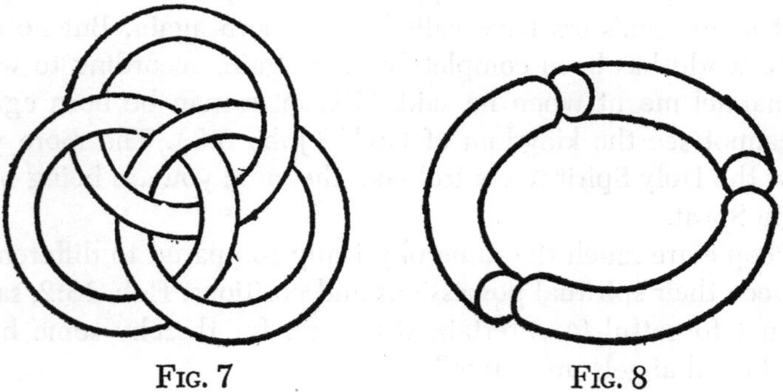

FIG. 7　　　　　　　　　　　　　　　FIG. 8

When the Holy Ghost third of a soul comes into his place for making a soul, he brings all the inherited knowledge which that soul will inherit. The soul of the lowest form of animal life is made of the Holy Ghost and nothing else. The next highest has both the Holy Ghost and the Spirit of Truth. Anything higher than a jellyfish has all three, as well as a spirit behind it. There are many spirits besides the Elect. The greatest evil living in the world is in the sea.

Some people have found out about this evil before they were born and for that reason are unable to eat certain seafood, because the taste is nothing but a knowledge of what is behind it. When they again acquire this knowledge through the sense of taste, it is too real and repulsive to tolerate.

When any animal life dies, the body gives up the Spirit of Love first, then the Spirit of Truth. However, it might still come back to life again and is not completely dead until it gives up the Ghost.

When a soul leaves this world, it goes back where it came from, unless it was born across the top of the first heaven. In that case you have three general routes to eternity as shown in Figure 9.

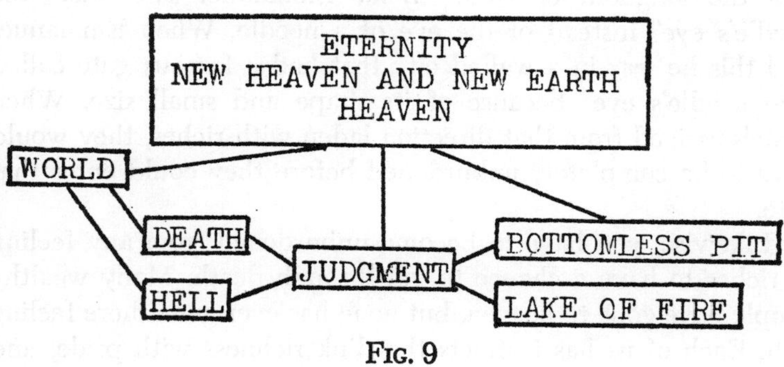

Fig. 9

When human babies die, they go back through heaven and to God. There are to be 144,000 people in heaven by the second coming of Christ.

When the average person dies, he starts back the way he came, but very few get through the spirit of this world. They remain in it completely unconscious. It is so hard to get through death that no one since Adam's time was able to do it, until

Emmanuel left a path. The ones who go to heaven get through in one of three ways, by carrying spiritual responsibility, by sacrifice, or by aiming straight at the truth.

The average person would have the best chance by aiming at the truth while backing up against it. But since life goes in a circle, it is possible to go to heaven by aiming at the truth by going forward at the time you die.

The one who do will see something very bright just before they leave this world. They may have time to comment on it, as it was reported Thomas Edison did just before he died. His kind don't go back through the spirit of this world but go forward.

It would take a lifetime of practice to go forward. But to go backwards you merely keep far enough away from pride and from any feeling connected with it, such as feeling rich.

Certain passages in the Bible may lead to the wrong conclusions regarding wealth, as in Mark 10:25: "It is easier for a camel to go through the eye of a needle. than for a rich man to enter into the kingdom of God." What Emmanuel said was "the needle's eye" instead of the eye of a needle. When Emmanuel said this he was in a walled city that had a famous gate called "the needle's eye" because of its shape and small size. When camels arrived from that direction laden with riches, they would have to be completely unburdened before they could enter that gate.

Likewise, you have to become unburdened from any feeling of riches to have a chance to get through death. Many wealthy people have gone to heaven, but none has ever gone there feeling rich. Each of us has instincts that link richness with pride, and pride is death.

The great majority go to death when they die, which is complete unconsciousness. If you have to stand before the judgment, then afterwards you will either go on to eternity, or the three parts of your soul will separate and return to their origin. The rest of your personality, which is made of nothing, will go into the Lake of Fire. Or, if you have what it takes to live forever but like worldly sensations better than you should in relation to other things, then the bottomless pit is available to correct this condition. There is no pain or unconsciousness here, but the strongest of the worldly sensations. One of the feelings in the bottomless pit is that of falling.

Even though each kind of trouble in the world has been made to do as much good as possible, there was still a need for lots of woe. From Adam's time to the second coming of Christ, there is so much trouble that some of the Elect, in looking at the trouble ahead, thought they would have to go through it in a way called *like a man.* Since the one who is patience is a member named Hugh, they also had to do it like a Hugh man. But this Hugh man (human) family is about to come to the end of this particular dispensation.

There are three tunnels that look like horns, arranged as in Figure 10.

 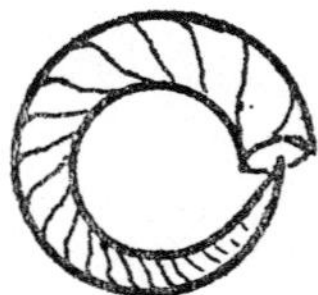

FIG. 10

The Spirit of Truth horn and the Holy Ghost horn are together. If you could get close enough to the point of the horn for the Spirit of Truth, you could do things that require insight and understanding. The better you like the truth, the closer to this point you are coming. To get past it, you would have to like the truth better than Emmanuel did when he was in this world, which is not likely.

If you could get past the point of the Holy Ghost horn, something physical would be involved here. You could make so much noise that everyone below the first heaven would hear it.

If you could remove the point from the center of the third horn, this would unlock the kingdom, and you could usher in the millennium. Going past the point in any one of these will disconnect it. When someone finally gets past the point of the

Spirit of Truth, there will then be "one down and two to go."
The Spirit of Truth is the most appropriate place to start. Learning how to think is more like learning first things first. When you
try hard to discover the truth and succeed, it will bring a feeling
of happiness, and happiness and truth are closely related.

The amount of happiness any person will have who lives
forever will be as much as that individual wants. Any more
would overflow. However, some will have a greater capacity
than others; each will have his own size cup for happiness.
There is a way to make your cup bigger, and now is the time
to do it.

20

Cup for Happiness

Your capacity for happiness, which the Bible calls your cup, is nothing more or less than how well you like the truth, and therein lies a vast difference in people. Liking the truth isn't viable in itself, but there is a means to greatly increase your desire for truth. The principle is explained by the saying "Your appetite grows on what it feeds." The more you try to determine the truth, the better you like it when you find it; the better you like the truth, the harder you will try to find it.

We all have inherited desires that go unnoticed until we begin to satisfy them. The more we feed our desires, the more prominent they become. When we try hard, it makes the feelings stronger when we succeed. By trying hard to find the truth about any subject, our desire for truth will grow with our success.

To use this principle let us take some questions that need answers, then aim at the truth for the answers. Some of the main problems of the nation today are crime, juvenile delinquency, the high divorce rate, industrial unrest, and the international situation which, it seems, is leading to war. Finding the answers is very important, to say the least.

Let's begin with the crime problem. The main thing to understand is the difference between a criminal and someone who is honest. A criminal behaves himself in order to escape punishment. The honest person obeys the law for one or more of several better reasons. When a criminal plans to rob a store but does not, because he notices policemen in the vicinity, he is just as much a criminal as if he had robbed the store. "For as he thinketh in his heart, so is he." If he stays home only because he is afraid he might get caught, he is still a criminal.

The highest motive for not taking something from someone

else is the unselfish feeling that the victim will then no longer have it. Unselfishness alone can make some behave. Another very good motive for being honest is a desire to have everything right. This desire might be partly acquired from proper upbringing, and partly inherited.

It is important, but not good for spiritual reasons, to feel proud of your honesty. And lastly, what the Bible calls the fear of the Lord is enough motivation for some.

No one should be made to feel he must behave only to escape punishment. When the very young misbehave, how are we going to make them behave through punishment, without instilling the idea that the reason they should mind is to avoid punishment? A hard question! Even so, punishment should always be the last resort. To go in the opposite direction and do nothing to guide them would also be an admission of failure.

On the positive side, the most important factor in rearing a child is the emotional attitude of the parents. The younger a child, the easier he can feel the motives of all those who have anything to do with him. When the desire is purely to help the child, the motive is valued so highly by the child that he will try as hard as he can to please. The Bible mentions the rod of correction or discipline. This rod, or spirit, should be used basically to help the child, of course, rather than to punish to vent your anger.

Children think many things are trivial, but when their instincts make them feel that certain things are important, the parents should never lie about or dodge these things. Otherwise, a permanent gulf between them will result. This is especially true of sex.

Sexual feelings would be stronger if sex were shrouded in more mystery. Also, the more important a subject seems, the stronger will be all feelings pertaining to it. The first mystery on the subject is likely to be the mystery of birth. The spiritual phenomenon here still leaves plenty of room for mystery. Your worldly body is just a place to live in now, so the question of from whence you came still remains.

The importance of the sexual side of life can be taught correctly, but only in the home. The parents themselves must be the example.

Sadly, when some parents were children, their sexual feelings and knowledge were associated with shame. This interferes with the teaching of their own children. Even more so do the decisions and ideals that some live by. Children should learn, among other things, to relate sexual feelings with the platonic love in marriage. The best and most natural time to impart sex education is when it is asked for.

Anyone in a position to influence children can make his own capacity for happiness greater by trying to influence the young wisely. Sometimes this will mean less supervision instead of more. If a child wants to trade toys, to him it might be big, important business. To raise him to become an executive, let him do it.

While this would help to reduce the future crime problem, the criminals today are already grown. What these types do not appreciate is that if your motive is complete selfishness, you would still have to do the same thing to get the best for yourself as if your motive were to follow the Ten Commandments and aim at the truth.

When a boy of five to ten years old listens to an older boy talking of the things he has done, the young one may set up this type of behavior as an ideal. Even when forgotten, it will make him try to act like the ideal he has adopted. There are no born criminals. It is possible to have ideals that are as low as the maligned snake in the grass. It is these ideals that account for much juvenile delinquency.

Magazine and newspaper reports show that vandalism is on the increase all over the world. Many youths like to break windows, damage automobiles, and do harm at random. To them it is like playing a trick on someone. The spirit behind practical jokes is responsible for more vandalism than is generally realized, almost all of it, in fact.

When you play a trick on someone, it almost always causes him some degree of trouble; otherwise, it would not be a trick. If a small amount of trouble is good, then a large amount should be better. That is the reasoning of many children. The younger and more sensitive a child, the more the damage that will be done by teaching him to enjoy practical jokes.

Practical jokes that are enjoyed by all the people involved really do the most harm. If it were not for the pleasing practical jokes, the whole habit would die out.

In the problem of happy marriage, the word *love* is often used too loosely. The ideal marriage is half sensual, half platonic, with as much of both as you can acquire.

Sensual love can be helped by cleanliness, appearances, pleasant manners, sex technique, and especially by adding more platonic love. Platonic love, which is the Spirit of Love feeling, can be turned on almost like a faucet. The reason is that everyone's ancestors always wanted what they tried to get. You now have those instincts. If you continually try to get something you will begin to want it even when there was no desire at the start. The more you try, the stronger the desire.

If a person felt no platonic love for the one to whom he was married, he could acquire some by trying to be helpful, by trying to make his partner happy.

When industry and labor meet for a conference, they should first make sure that everyone understands elementary economics, in this case the relationship between four things: the total number of jobs in the nation; the total amount of money in use; the speed of circulation of money; and the average earnings. When one of these goes up or down, at least one of the other three will have to change along with it. To make more jobs in the nation, you would have to add more money to all the money in use, or have each person hold his pay for a shorter time before he spends it, or lower the wages so that each dollar represents more work.

Conversely, to make fewer jobs in the nation, you would have to take money out of use, slow its speed of circulation, or raise wages. Higher wages by themselves would cause unemployment, but if wages rose enough to put one million men out of work, and at the same time the speed of money in circulation rose enough to put two million men back to work, the net result would be one million more jobs. And those two go together, for the simple reason that people want to hurry and buy when wages are rising, because prices are rising, too.

By themselves, lower wages would produce more jobs, but when wages start down prices do, too. Nobody wants to buy now when he knows he can buy more next week at a lower price. The slower circulation of money causes more loss of jobs than the lower wages produce.

To help understand this, take an imaginary situation involving twelve men shipwrecked on an island. They first divide all their money equally and find they have ten dollars apiece. Each then goes to work and makes things to sell to the others. If wages are ten dollars a day, each may hold his wages for one day before buying something and still have full employment. If wages are only one dollar a day, wages may be held for an average of ten days without causing any unemployment. They could not spend it faster, for there would be nothing left to buy.

If a few more men arrived and wanted jobs, it would be necessary to add more money, lower the wages, or speed up its circulation. All credit can be classified as either adding more money or speeding up the circulation of money.

There is a nationwide labor problem in which labor, management, and government argue over working hours, a closed shop, wages, and unemployment. Resulting disagreements cause many strikes.

The way by which these strikes could be prevented is to divide the authority among the three of them so that any one of them could make a decision without requiring agreement from the other two. Allow labor to determine its own working hours, management to do the hiring and firing, and have any dispute over wage and fringe benefits settled by the third party—the government. With each having total authority in its own category, there would be few reasons to strike.

Wages need to be kept down in relation to the total amount of money in use, in order for the normal speed of circulation to provide plenty of jobs. In the years following the Second World

War, there was a general shortage of labor. If the government could prevent wages from rising in such times, there would always be a shortage of labor.

The problem of preventing war is becoming more important as the weapons become more terrible. Not many people have much to say about whether their nation goes to war or not. But a study of what heads of nations say to each other during the time preceding war will show that if personal or national pride had not been factors, the world would not have been thrown into conflict.

This world will remain tragic as long as pride is at work in it. It is no accident that pride is here now. Pride causes so much trouble it forces everyone to try to find an alternate way of life. Without this, we would not have developed our desire to gain the truth.

When it comes to trying hard to think straight, a common habit of thinking—which in turn is responsible for many mistakes—is to compare what is only partly similar without noticing the difference. Consider these three cases. Dwellers move from old houses that have high ceilings and are not insulated, into new houses with low ceilings and that are insulated. The high ceiling with the difficulty of heating is compared with the low ceilings and the ease of heating. So the high ceilings are mistakenly blamed.

A more common mistake is to compare the high wages and living standards of the present, with the lower wages and living standard of the past. If we reverted to the same means of production used one hundred years ago—by doing away with electric motors and laborsaving machinery—the living standard would drop back to what it was then, even if wages went up to one hundred dollars a day. Many people correlate our current high wages with the present high living standard, and the relatively lower wages of the past with their lesser standards. There is no connection, so no comparison should be made.

A more serious case is the relatively higher moral standards and large number of mental patients in the United States, compared to the difference in moral standards and lack of psychotics among the Polynesians. The mental breakdowns in the United States are so numerous that a search has been made in every direction for the prevention of mental disorders. By comparing it to the South Seas way of living, some have thought that would be a better way to live. The correct way to find answers is to look at causes.

Many mental cases have nothing to do with sex, but there are people who made strong decisions about behaving themselves when they were very young. A strong decision at that time can lead to a very strong influence the rest of their lives. Also, you have inherited more moral traits than you have immoral traits, and they are now a part of you. The way to keep out of a mental hospital is to live in harmony with yourself.

Aiming at the truth not only helps prevent mental trouble, but if you are successful enough it will produce a happy, free feeling. A love for the truth can be developed by diligently seeking it. You might experience some of this feeling by studying the solutions that someone else believes to be right.

Telling others how to think presumes that you know how yourself. To make such a claim is like the boy who claimed that once he made a great leap, and had witnesses to prove it. The one to whom he was speaking said, "Never mind the witnesses," as he drew a line on the ground. "Start from here and let's see you leap." So why not take mundane problems of universal interest and show the answers here.

21

Practical Ideas

When a person states his conclusions without giving provable reasons for them, he should at least offer some substantiation. Creation, the behavior of atoms, problems of time, and the like require complicated explanations. The topics are unfamiliar to the average person and are inadequately treated even here. For that reason it seems a good idea to solve some problems with which everyone is more or less familiar. The reader can then use his own ability to aim at the truth and draw his own conclusions in comparison.

For example, if you could have any design you wished, for a house, an automobile, plane, boat, or train, which design would be the best? I was able to think of the ideas in this chapter because of the feeling that goes with truth.

Let's begin with the house and decide which plan is the most livable. Many persons have very strong ideas about how they want their houses to look and one plan cannot satisfy everybody.

Houses can be built in sections in a factory where they can be made almost entirely by machinery, which would result in a low cost per housing unit. The sections could be transported by rail or truck and assembled at the site.

The house should be designed as a machine to live in. However, a three-view drawing would show it to be rather conventional-looking as in Figure 11.

Sunshine is a more penetrative form of heat than most, so it results in a more enjoyable feeling, besides being free. A house should be designed to utilize the heat from the sun. One way is to mount the entire house on a turntable with the highest side made of insulating glass (several panes spaced apart). A

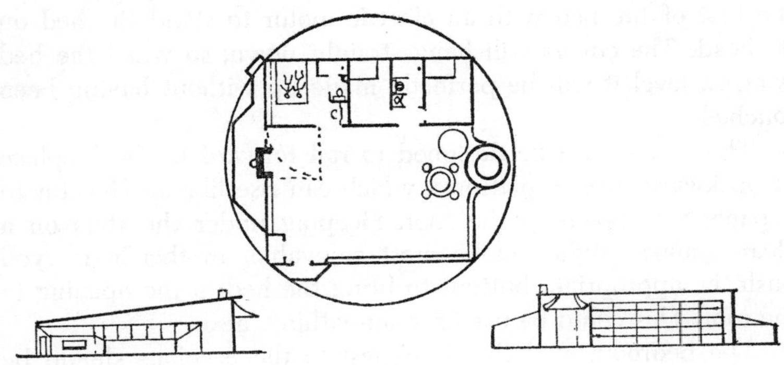

Fig. 11

small motor could be geared to rotate the house once every twenty-four hours, a larger one to rotate it to a new position when any change is desired. This source of heat should be supplemented by other sources of heat. An insulating curtain can be used on cold nights.

There are several ways of having self-cleaning floors. One would be to have a wall-to-wall carpet where the carpet rolls up on a spindle at one side of the room and with a machine to clean it as it rolls up. It could be placed out of sight under the floor. An electric motor could roll it and unroll it, leaving it rolled up when a hard floor is desired.

For the garage and workshop, a floor could be made of a fine, open grid where any dirt will fall into long bins with a conveyor belt at the bottom. With this design, plus air-cleaning equipment, there need be practically no dust or dirt.

Wall space not occupied by doors or windows can contain shelves. The doors that cover the shelves can resemble paneled walls.

The parents' bedroom should contain a bed of about 6 by 9 feet with an air mattress that gives control of air pressure on the individual tubes. This would allow for high pressure in the center and two outside tubes, with the rest at lower pressure. It could be a soft mattress on one side of the bed and hard on the other, if tastes differ. The covers should be clamped down at the foot of the bed with an electric motor to stand the bed on its head. The covers will hang straight down, so when the bed is again level it will be perfectly made up without having been touched.

The bed should be designed to roll forward to the fireplace or backwards over a platform, which can rise like an elevator to a panel that opens in the roof. Sleeping under the stars on a clear summer night can be most enjoyable. In this house you push the appropriate buttons to bring the bed to the opening in the roof. This could be used for sunbathing, also.

The bedroom wall that is closest to the fireplace should be double and hinged to swing over, so the fireplace will then be a part of the bedroom. On a stormy night with the bed rolled forward, you are then in front of a campfire. There are various interesting ways to use adjustable walls other than shown in Figure 11.

The fireplace chimney should contain a self-cleaning heat-exchange unit. This unit would take the heat from the smoke and warm the fresh air coming into the house. It would be built as shown in Figure 12.

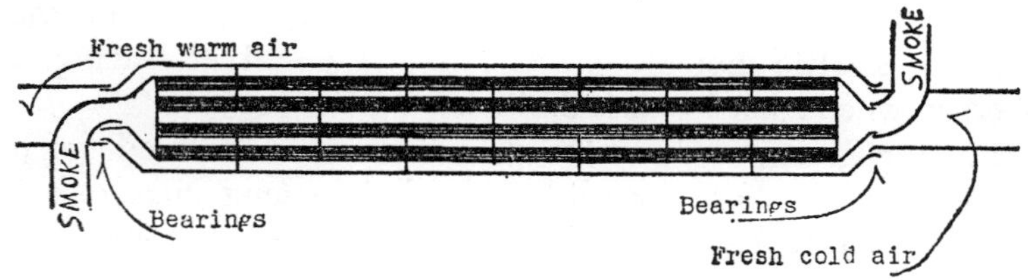

Fig. 12

The smoke would go out through long tubes that would normally become choked with soot, but here each tube contains a flat rod and the entire unit is rotated a few revolutions per hour by a small motor. The flat rods will continually slide down the sides of the tubes and keep them clean.

Where wood is available the fireplace should be automatically fed. An efficient way would be for the wood to be pushed up under the fire as needed so gases from the hot wood would come up through the fire. Add a trap door at one side for the ashes. To load the fireplace use a tube that comes in through the back of the fireplace and equipped with a fireproof door on top where it projects back into the woodshed (Figure 13).

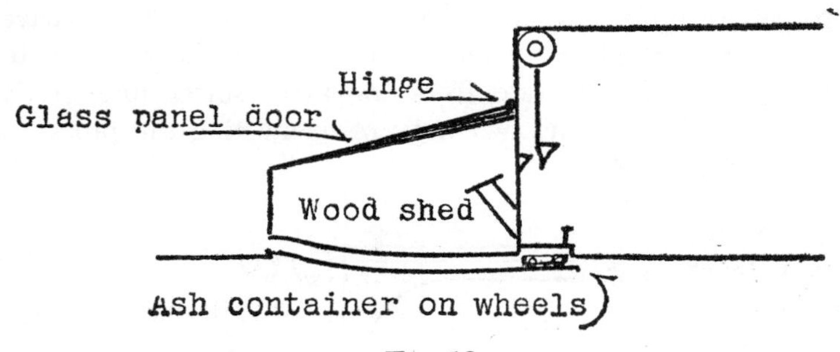

Fig. 13

The woodshed is designed so that the wood will dry without having to be stacked. A glass roof will make it hot enough to dry quickly. The glass roof is also the door. The house can be turned until the woodshed faces the driveway so that a truck can dump in a load of wood.

The kitchen has a large turntable containing stove, refrigerator, dishwasher, sink, and everything necessary for food preparation and clean-up. All rotate past a swivel chair used by the cook.

When this swivel chair is turned one-third of a revolution it faces a worktable featuring mixing machines, cooking utensils and the like which also rotate above the working surface.

The pancake-making machine would resemble two band saws backed up against each other, with wide bands that nearly touch. The batter would pour in between the two bands as they slowly traveled downward. With heat applied to the opposite side of both bands, the pancakes would cook twice as fast; and could be from very thin and all crust, to very thick, depending on the adjustment.

When the swivel chair is rotated the next third of the way, it faces the dining table. The dining table contains two rotating surfaces. The outside surface is about one foot wide and is rotated slowly until the plates and silverware are put in place. The rest of the table continues to turn slowly during the meal and can be stopped by anyone sitting at the table.

The part of the kitchen that contains the dishwasher would have water supplied from a pipe in the center with a swivel joint and packing gland. It may be desirable to keep the water supply completely separate from the main sewer line in the center of the house. The two ways of connecting the pipes are shown in Figure 14.

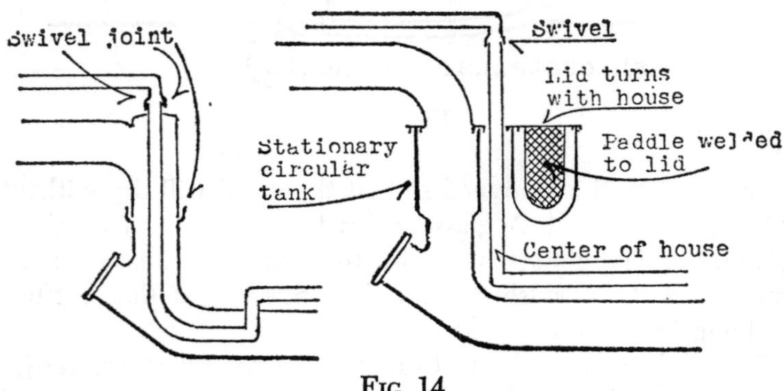

Fig. 14

Bathrooms should contain one extra piece of sanitary equipment, for there is a way general health can be greatly improved without much added expense. The skin is a very important eliminating organ. A healthy skin action would increase the general health more than any other single thing. A healthy skin simply means that the blood comes close to the surface very easily.

A bathtub of warm water stimulates the blood to this effect, but the reaction from any stimulant is slightly opposite from the first action and tends to be permanent. The best is a scrubbing machine combined with a shower with water more cool than warm.

A simple design would be a square shaft standing to the front of the shower with an electric motor to rotate the shaft one-quarter turn back and forth, with a cross arm that can slide up and down the shaft. A long, rough towel would be fastened to each end of the cross arm and around the person using it. There is no excuse to wait for a machine to scrub you, muscle will do with the towel dipped in water. This would be preventive medicine. Another very important one would be drinking enough water.

Housekeeping in this dwelling would not provide enough exercise. A superb source of exercise is swimming. All swimming pools should have safety features, such as a wire net that remains at the bottom when the pool is in use. When a person is in trouble, the net could be raised underneath him. When the pool is not in use, the net could be left at the top of the pool above the water. To prevent anyone from diving in when the net is up, there should be a fence around the edge of the water that would rise with the net.

A satisfactory swimming pool design for the average family is a pool that is deep at one end for diving, shallow at the other for wading, with a gradually inclined bottom. The net would be hinged at the shallow end at the surface of the water. The net at the deep end is all that would need to be raised to bring it level with the surface of the water. The fence would be high at the deep end and low at the shallow end.

The diving board could be mounted on a turntable and be used as a crank for raising the net. When the diving board is turned away from the swimming pool, the net would be up. If the climate is cold enough for ice skating, the net could be brought up directly under the surface for the winter.

If your plot is 100 by 100, the house, garage, and swimming pool might be laid out as in Figure 15.

The best reason for having fruit trees, a berry patch, and a small garden is so these foods can be eaten as soon as they are picked. Being still alive, they will give you extra energy. One likely place for a garden is on a flat roof. A roof that is flat, or nearly flat, should be put to use for something besides a roof.

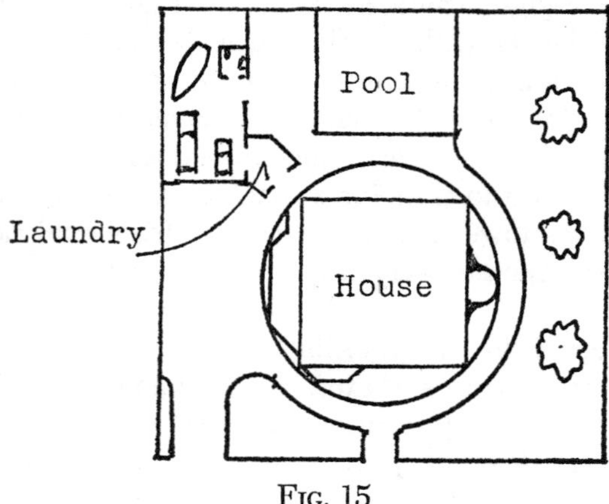

FIG. 15

It should be built strong enough to support a thin layer of soil for a garden; soil is also good insulation. If the roof is used for a garden, an automatic cultivator could be guided by rails to condition the soil and keep the garden weed-free automatically.

Another use for a flat roof would be as a port for a helicopter. Folding walls and roof of a hangar could lie flat until the helicopter landed; then the walls and roof could fold up and over the aircraft. A flat roof, of course, is only practical for a climate with no heavy snow.

The garage should be placed so that the south wall faces the swimming pool, if possible. The south wall should be hollow, then filled with dirt and with holes large enough for strawberry plants to grow out the side.

The garage could have a workshop or hobby room at one end. A folding bed could make it into a guest room. The lavatory could also be used by those at the swimming pool, without their having to track through the house. There would be room for a trailer in the garage, as well as two cars.

So much money is spent in America on cars that a closer look should be taken at this expense. A large part of the wasted money is spent on new models because of changing body styles.

When there was a trend towards building lower cars, a simple and popular way was to use smaller wheels. Yet if the wheel diameter were increased fifty percent, the tire mileage would increase not fifty percent but several hundred percent. There are three reasons for this, besides the extra wearing surface of the tire. With a larger diameter, the angle between the flat spot (where the tire is in contact with the road) and the rest of the tire is proportionately less. Two, the angle is changed less rapidly. Three, it is changed a fewer number of times. These factors will cause less heat to be generated, and heat has been proven to be the main cause of tire wear. A large wheel makes small bumps out of large ones, and is less likely to skid.

If a car flew through the air like an airplane, the part that would cause the most wind resistance would be the underside of the car, far more than grille or windshield. Yet when it travels on the road, the underside has even more wind resistance than if it flew. The reason is that air not only sticks to the car; it also sticks to the road. So, the underside of a car should be perfectly smooth, with only the wheels protruding.

If a modern car had large wheels, high pressure tires, and a smooth underside, it might double the miles per gallon for high-way driving, even with today's inefficient engines.

While economy is a continual problem, it is safety that requires immediate attention. There should be safer cars, highways, and drivers.

All cars should have governors that would prevent any speed above a maximum speed that is set for the roads and highways of the entire nation. It is too easy for a driver to go much faster than he thinks he is driving. There should be a speedometer with numbers about two inches high and located just above the radiator, so the driver could see it without making such a radical change in the direction and focus of his eyes.

The safest brakes would be correctly designed mechanical brakes. One argument against the hydraulic variety is the many times that brake fluid has been lost. Brakes designed as in Figure 16 would distribute the power applied to the brake pedal equally to each wheel, just as well as is done by hydraulic brakes, and much more safely.

If one or more mechanical brakes fail, the car will still have

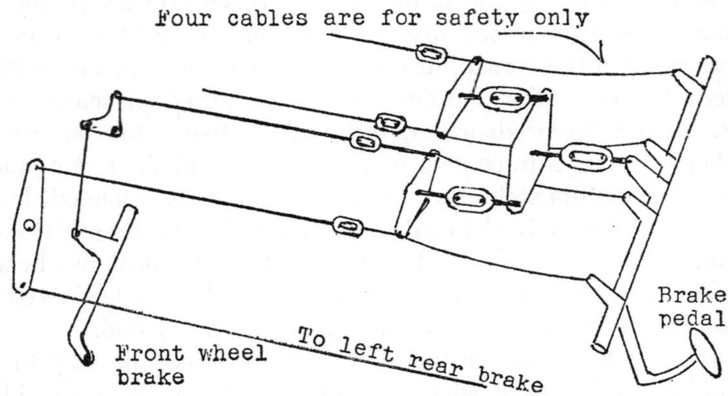

FIG. 16

the remaining brakes. This system can be inspected any time the hood is raised. Adjustment for slack would be easy to make but seldom needed. The bolts or clevis pins should be about three times bigger than those used in old cars. Hydraulic brakes do not transmit more power from your foot to the brakes. Pumping them up merely takes the slack out, which may have to be done at the same time the brakes are unexpectedly needed.

Highways should have a curved center strip that would eliminate head-on collisions, as in Figure 17.

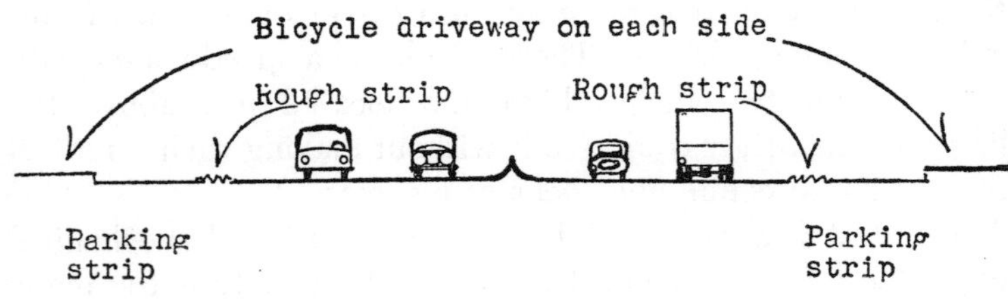

FIG. 17

The center strip would turn back sleeping drivers who ran up on it, and the rough strip at the side would jolt them awake.

There are many other ways to improve safety, but the greatest improvement will have to come from the drivers themselves.

Anyone learning to drive should realize that he probably has lifetime habits that will influence his driving, unless he becomes conscious of them. A person may be told at an early age that he should always do his duty and not try to avoid something just because he doesn't like it. If it is an arithmetic problem, he should not slow down but keep going until he gets past it. If he adopts this as an ideal, it will cause a desire to steer around any trouble he sees ahead, whereas he should slow down, even stop, sometimes. This causes more trouble while learning than it does later.

When reaching a door at the same time as a man, women can be accustomed to going ahead. This lifetime habit of going ahead must not be applied to driving a car.

Some have the habit of expressing mental frustrations in a physical way. The angrier some people get, the faster and more recklessly they drive. When the problems caused by alcohol (called wormwood in the book of Revelation) are overcome, in many cases, it will be with spiritual help. The principle of getting this help is mentioned in John 16:24: "Ask, and ye shall receive."

Where speed is needed, a different vehicle altogether should be used. A flying automobile, or "roadable airplane," is neither a good automobile nor a good airplane. But an airplane that can land on a roof is quite desirable. A convertiplane is an old idea, still undeveloped. If the private planes of the most popular type in use today were converted for vertical takeoff and landing, they would resemble that shown in Figure 18.

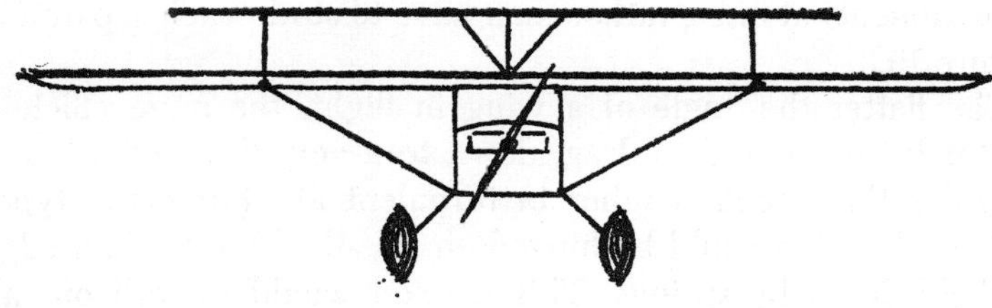

FIG. 18

While the craft was used as an airplane, the rotor would remain stationary. Small jets at the rotor tips would be used for takeoff. To stop the rotor in the air, the jets would be rotated 180 degrees. A freewheeling device would allow the rotor to turn freely one way but very slow in reverse, until it was lined up with the wing where short struts would swing up and lock it in position. This would be done automatically so the pilot would need only to push a button to stop the rotor.

A wing with a leading edge exactly the same as the trailing edge and with the thickest part of the wing in the center can be satisfactory. The rotor would be of this design, because one side is flying backwards when it is held stationary.

A photograph of the instrument panel of an airplane, especially a large one, will show a maze of instruments with needles pointing in every direction. A better design, and one which would give a pilot more time to look elsewhere, would be instruments about one inch wide and eight inches high placed as close together as possible. Each indicator should be a short bar that moves vertically. Each instrument should have an adjustable scale so that the proper setting will be in the center.

For example, if the pilot wishes to cruise at five thousand feet, he adjusts the scale on the altimeter so that the five-thousand-foot mark is in the center. The rate of climb indicator should show zero in the center. With the oil pressure, oil temperature, cylinder temperature, and all gauges properly adjusted, the pilot has merely to glance quickly at his instrument panel. If everything is working correctly, the indicator bar on each instrument will be in the center, and all together will look like a straight line across the panel. In this way the pilot can check all instruments at once, rather than have to study each separately (Figure 19).

The flatter the angle of a wing in flight, the more efficient it is for lift compared to drag, down to a very flat angle; but it also rides that much rougher in turbulent air. For many types of plane the wing could be hinged on ahead of the leading edge and held down by springs. This method would smooth out all bumps. The wing would be locked in place for takeoff and landing.

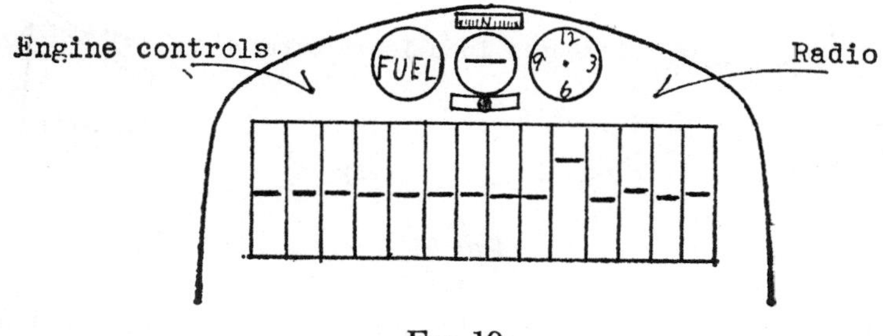

FIG. 19

This is also a method by which it is possible to build a glider that will fly better than a buzzard, because the wings are more flexible. When an upward air current forces the wing up against the pull of the springs, the energy is stored in the springs. When the wing is pulled down, that energy is used for propulsion. Also, when the wing is pushed up, it is pointing down, which allows the upward air current to accelerate the plane instead of creating a bumpy ride. There are many possible ways to make a flexible wing glider. One practical way is shown in Figure 20.

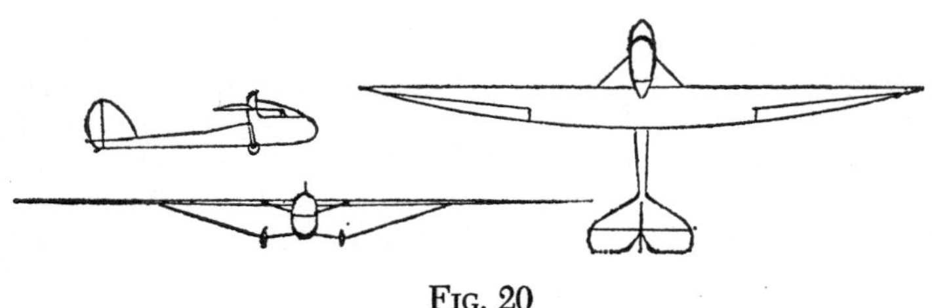

FIG. 20

The wing is hinged to swing around a pivot in front of the cockpit. This is not only strong, but it allows the pilot to keep track of the wing position while looking ahead. Two rollers in the wing would roll up and down on a guide located behind the pilot.

Springs would have the effect of pulling the wing down from each side and the center. The struts should be rigged so that one side of the wing cannot go up or down without the other. Two cables and six pulleys would do it as shown in Figure 21.

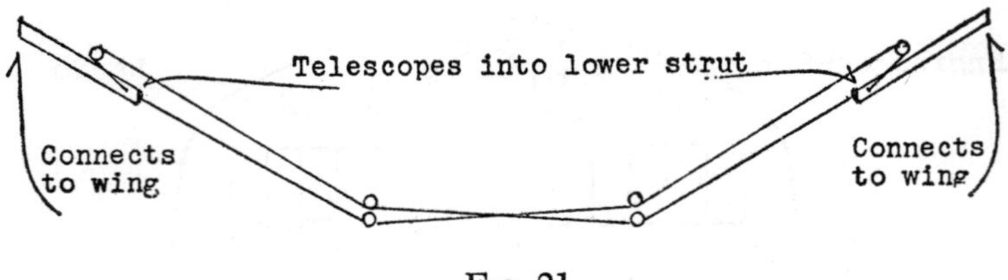

FIG. 21

When flying with or against a gusty wind, the springs that hold the wing will store up more energy if the wing travels all the way up when it is struck head-on by a sudden gust. But the wing will not travel up if it immediately points down as it starts up. On the other hand, if the wing is flying through vertical air currents, then it should point down as it goes up. The pilot should have a control crank to adjust the wing behavior for the best performance (Figure 22).

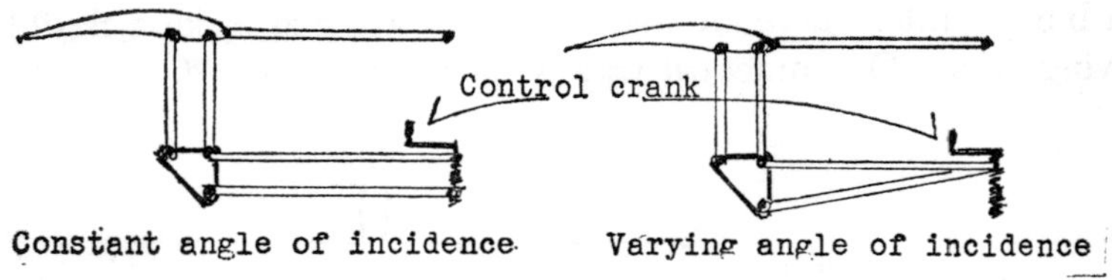

FIG. 22

The wing should also have a flexible trailing edge that would adjust itself according to the load.

A motorless propeller with blades that fold straight back could be retracted into the nose of this glider. When extended it would have a dual purpose. With adjustable pitch control the blades could be flattened so they would spin like a rotor. In this way the propeller would have as much drag as a parachute of the same diameter and could be used as an air brake. With a jet at each blade tip the propeller would take the place of a tow plane for takeoff.

A better wheel for planes with fixed landing gear would

consist of three separate tires built together with the sides filled in with sponge rubber (Figure 23).

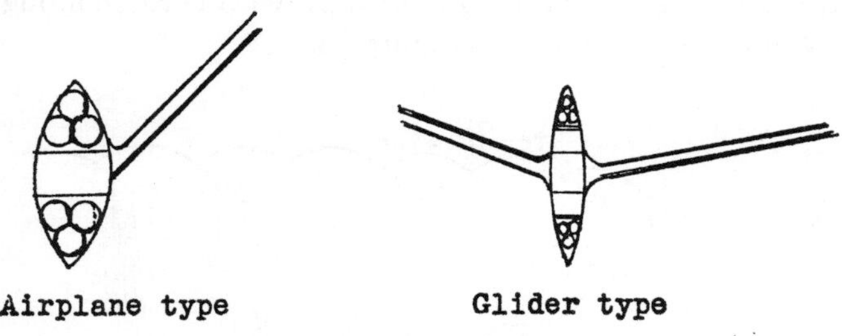

Fig. 23

Each tire could be manufactured separately like a one-piece bicycle tire and vulcanized together with a plastic rim. When it becomes too badly worn or damaged, the whole thing could be thrown away. Punctures could be fixed by the hollow-needle method of squirting a puddle of rubber cement straight up through the puncture.

Weight has always been a consideration in designing airplanes. If a person wanted to fly among billowing white clouds on a warm summer day for the sheer fun of flying, the best plane for the purpose might be an extremely lightweight, open-type plane with a slow and nearly silent propeller. If this plane is as light as possible, it will look like Figure 24.

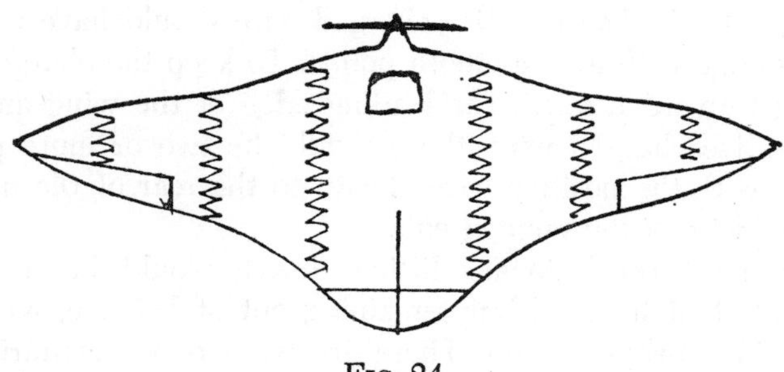

Fig. 24

It would be made of a material such as balloon cloth. Where the wing is thin, it could be made of one layer and of several layers where the wing is thick. It would contain no spars or ribs but would hold its shape by air pressure with cords holding the top and bottom together as in Figure 25.

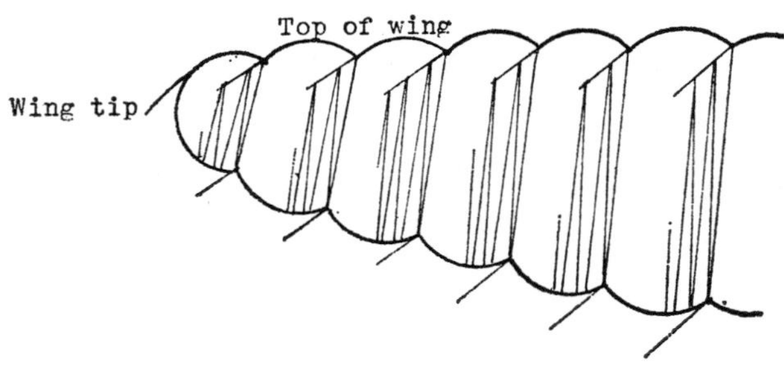

Fig. 25

With a rigid-type of construction, and if built in large sizes, this design would also be good for carrying heavy loads.

Wind resistance can be nearly eliminated by an electrical method based on discoveries made in the early days of electrical experimenting. By placing pairs of flat wires close together and from wing tip to wing tip, with the front wire of every pair carrying a negative charge, the rear carrying a positive charge, there will be a flow through the air called an electric wind.

The wires should be bonded to the wing surface and the space between them filled with plastic, so that the wing surface will be smooth. The negative-charged wire should have a sharp trailing edge with fine sawtooth points. To keep the charge from flowing forward towards the leading edge of the wing and the last positive charged wire, there should be two or more power sources with the positive wire always to the rear of the nearest negative wire of the same circuit.

The most revolutionary lifting device would be a wheel spinning at high speed but remaining out of balance, with the heavy side always on top. There are ways of momentarily exchanging weight and energy so that weight changed into energy at the bottom could be put back on top as weight. The lift would be independent of the atmosphere.

Despite their glamour, spacecraft are not very important compared to ordinary load-carrying aircraft. Flying heavy loads over water could compete with boats. A simple design for a better ship would be a very large flat-bottomed vessel with a scow-shaped bow and stern. The bow, stern, and sides should be about three feet lower than the bottom, so that when air is pumped under, it cannot escape. The air would force the water down until it was even with the bow, stern, and sides. The bottom would then remain entirely dry. No more power would be needed to pump air underneath, for the air would be trapped there.

To prevent the air from rushing across to one side and allowing the boat to tip, there should be a keel down the center that would just touch the water. To help the bow and stern remain level, another scow-shaped bulge should extend down from the bottom and run across from one side to the other at the center of the ship. If it barely touched the water, this would prevent the air from rushing from one end to the other.

If very high speed is desired, a sheet of air could be blown under the bow at the waterline, through a gill extending all the way across. Since the air is at a higher pressure under the ship than outside, and since no more air is needed underneath, the same air could be pumped back through the gill. The boat would not have much resistance because the entire bottom would be floating on air.

Hovercraft already in use for years support themselves on air blown underneath faster than it can escape, but they require too much horsepower for heavy freight. A boat with more conventional lines would also benefit from gills that maintain a sheet of air between its hull and the water. The top of such a ship should look like the back of a salmon. It should have more horsepower than conventional ships, but it would get there so much faster that it would not use any more fuel.

To get the most enjoyment from a pleasure boat, you should build it yourself. There is much happiness caused by using skill.

Also, building it makes you appreciate the boat more; you become acquainted with its "personality." This feeling can be so strong that there is some danger of worshipping the things you make with your hands.

There is particular pleasure in using power that is free, as in a sailboat. A sail, however, is not the most efficient way to harness the wind. A large windmill with controllable-pitch blades could drive an underwater propeller that would give the craft greater speed. For stability, a small boat could use twin hulls, a principle widely used in catamarans. No matter how big the boat, there would be no crew to handle sails, and the boat could run in any direction, including straight into the wind, which would create additional wind power.

Sailing ships for cargo could almost make a comeback, by using this windmill design. When no wind is blowing, an auxiliary motor could be used. Old-time sailboats had to tack to travel against the wind, requiring a large crew to man the sails. This design would eliminate both tacking and crew.

When a motor is used, the most efficient propulsion for boats is an airplane-type propeller. It might be noisy, windy, expensive or dangerous, but still the most efficient. Even for slower ships built for cargo a large slow-turning air propeller would be more efficient than a marine propeller. For a propeller blade to be the most efficient, it should be shaped like a wing by being long and narrow, which would be too weak for a marine propeller.

Load-carrying on land can be greatly improved. Railroads are potentially the most efficient for distances greater than a few miles. The railroads would have to be allowed to use every labor-saving method they could find, however, and one big improvement would be a better track.

The only argument in favor of wooden ties that I can find is that rails need resilience wherever the track is rough. But the roughness was caused by the weakness of the ties in the first place.

With wheels that have no flat spots and with a smooth track, any resilience needed should be in the wheels. One method is the spring-wheel type of suspension as shown in Figure 26.

Fig. 26

If there is any vibration it will be absorbed by the shape of the spokes. Extra heavy-duty tires with steel wire cord would also do, as in Figure 27.

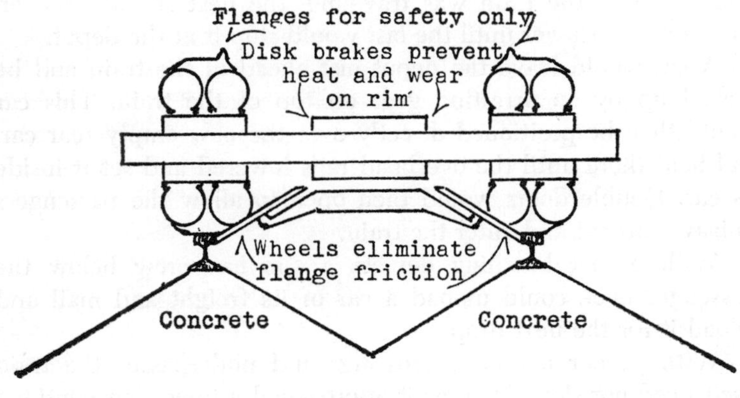

Fig. 27

When tires are used on a highway, they touch only on the bottom of the tire. But if they were used on a railroad, they would be supported by a rim that not only would fit their circumference but also the cross section. For that reason they would support a very much greater load.

An air hose connected to the tires through the center of the hub would maintain constant air pressure. Steel side plates from the inside rim would overlap those from the outside rim so the tires would not be exposed to damage and would be blowout-proof.

Considerable labor could be saved by replacing wooden ties with a concrete ridge under each rail.

If railroads were to approach their utimate efficiency, one change would be double-decker trains, passengers on the upper deck and mail, parcel post and freight of moderate bulk on the lower.

When a passenger on this train approached his destination, he would walk back to the last car, which would be a car within a car. This car would have wheels above its roof that would engage overhead rails, beginning about one mile from the depot. These rails would be inclined so they would slowly lift this car above the rest of the train. A row of wheels with rubber tires would press down on the roof. The first wheel would spin at the same velocity the train was traveling, the next slightly slower, and each one slower until the last would stop it at the depot.

A car would leave the depot just ahead of the train and be picked up by an arresting gear on top of the train. This car would then be positioned directly over the now empty rear car, and held there until the overhead rails lowered and set it inside its car. Double doors would then open to allow the passengers to leave this car and enter the train.

With proper handling devices a one-man crew below the passenger deck could unload a car of its freight and mail and reload it for the next drop.

With proper overhead crossings and underpasses the train itself need not slow down as it approached a town, but continue on across the country at a uniform speed, with a consequent saving in fuel and time.

Engines used to power trains, boats, planes, and cars are known to be very wasteful of fuel. They may not average twenty-five percent efficiency. What would these engines look like if they had the ability to run at a much higher efficiency?

Turbine power will be used much more generally, and so the turbine should be of general interest. In a gas turbine a compressor compresses air in which fuel is burned. The expanding air runs a turbine, the turbine runs the compressor, and what power is left over is the useful power of the turbine.

Heat is a form of energy. Yet the exhaust of a gas turbine holds much heat, even after a heat exchange unit (called a regenerator) is used. Any heat in the exhaust is wasted power. To understand how a gas turbine can be made more efficient, it should be understood that when air is compressed it gets hotter; when it expands it gets colder.

The highest possible efficiency can be reached by compressing air to a certain pressure without allowing its temperature to rise. That is, use a cooling system to take heat out of the air as it is compressed. Then its temperature should be allowed to rise with the compression until its peak pressure is reached. On the power stroke the opposite should take place. The air should expand against a working surface (either a piston or turbine blades) to a certain pressure while the temperature remains the same. That is, a heater should be used to put heat into the air as it expands so that the temperature remains the same until it reaches a certain pressure. Then, both the temperature and pressure should be allowed to drop together, so that when it reaches its original pressure it will also be at its original temperature. That complete cycle is called the Carnot cycle; theoretically, it reaches the highest possible efficiency of any engine working within the same temperature limits.

A turbine designed as in Figure 28 would roughly duplicate the Carnot cycle and would be more efficient than those now in use.

After the air is compressed by each compressor except the last one, it passes through the cooler. From the last compressor it goes to the burner.

The burner for this engine would build up some added pressure all by itself. The burner would fire first on one side, then on the other. Each side would create a jet-type of pump that would draw out the burnt gases and draw in a fresh charge for the other side. Each time the fresh charge would reach the white-hot end of the burner, it would fire.

After the air had left the burner at high temperature, it would

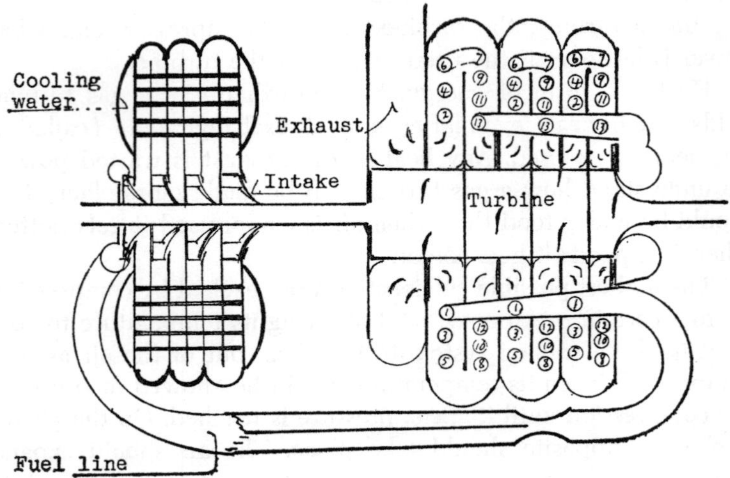

FIG. 28

be divided into equal parts for each of the three heaters. The heaters would receive their heat from this air. The air would leave at a lower temperature and go to the high pressure end of the turbine, all the air going through all of the turbine. After it had passed through the first or high pressure row of turbine blades, it would be reheated for each succeeding row. It should be exhausted at nearly the same temperature and pressure as when it entered the compressors.

The advantage in cooling the gases before they enter the turbine, then picking up the same heat again after each succeeding stage, is that extremely high compression may be used without heat too great for metal to tolerate.

The turbine blades should be designed to hold the air back as much as possible. Slower moving air, depending on pressure instead of velocity, would mean less loss of power through friction. The drawing of the tubes in Figure 28 is simplified to show the principle more clearly.

An efficient engine is one that uses some method of changing a large part of the heat into mechanical work, such as the design shown in Figure 29.

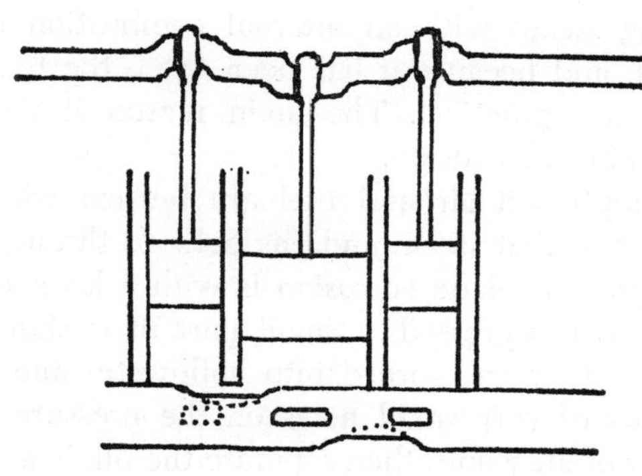

Fig. 29

The two outside cylinders are four-cycle gas or Diesel; the center cylinder is two-cycle steam. The two four-cycle cylinders are water-cooled by pumping the water around each cylinder and into a small tank until it reaches the right temperature. Instead of sending it to a radiator, it is sprayed into these cylinders on each power stroke. This will not only cause these cylinders to develop more power and keep the engine from overheating, but the exhaust gas will be mostly steam that will discharge into the center cylinder.

The valve assembly consists of a large hollow tube geared to turn at one-half crankshaft speed. The incoming air or gas enters this tube. An opening near each end of the tube acts as an inlet valve for the cylinder at that end. Two cup-shaped indentations allow the exhaust to travel from the end cylinders to the center cylinder, and a short oblong tube runs across, acting as the exhaust for the steam cylinder.

With this type of valve the engine would need to burn a fuel that would not cause carbon, and it would have to be made of metal that would neither rust nor corrode.

The engine might be thought of as a one-cylinder steam engine with a boiler on each side. All the heat not only would go into the steam, but the boilers would deliver considerable power to the crankshaft directly. The engine should be inverted to allow excess water to drain out.

Combining steam with an internal combustion engine is a very old idea, and because it has been tried, the tendency is to believe it is not practical. The main reason it has not been successful has been corrosion.

When compressed air and fuel are burned while water is sprayed into it so that steam and gas both go through a turbine, one way to prevent blade corrosion is with a layer of clean air. After the air is compressed, a small part of it should be compressed still further and forced into hollow turbine blades that have hundreds of very small holes on the pressure side of the blade. A layer of air would then separate the blade and the working gases. This air would also help run the turbine, and the power required to compress it not wasted.

Another way of using the exhaust after the cooling water has been sprayed inside the cylinder, would be with a cam instead of a crank on the main shaft. It would be possible to have the piston travel a normal inlet and compression stroke, and then a very long power stroke. The exhaust stroke should travel all the way to the top for complete removal of exhaust gases. The cylinders could be placed parallel to the shaft, making a very compact engine.

A lack of money for research partly explains the slow progress in science and invention. A more important reason is executives with the wrong personality for the job. When very high salaries are paid, many persons try to get the job. The ones with the most salesmanship are more likely to sell the company on the idea of hiring them. Seldom do salesmanship and inventive ability go together.

If the automobile industry had used more imagination, they would have long ago developed a car with a small diesel engine placed in back, to drive the rear wheels, and a much larger gasoline engine in front, to drive the front wheels. It would be the most reliable car ever made, as well as the most versatile, and with the best fuel economy.

The amount of money necessary to develop a new car or engine, will depend on inventive ability far more than on anything else.

A practical, high efficiency engine for automobiles would be a combination gasoline and hot-air engine. The hot-air side would run on the wasted heat from both the exhaust and the cooling system of the gasoline engine.

In order to get the most heat into the exhaust from the least amount of fuel, the gasoline engine should be air-cooled by having vertical fins up the side of the cylinder. A jacket over these fins would have an overhead inlet valve in the center of the cylinder head. On the inlet stroke the air would be sucked up the sides and into the cylinder. The heat from the cooling system would also be in the exhaust gas. The exhaust valve should be L-head with the exhaust gas going directly to the heater of the hot-air engine, or into the cylinder containing the working piston.

As a gasoline engine only, this design would be slightly less efficient than a modern automobile engine. As a low compression Diesel it would be slightly more efficient than a gasoline engine. In either case, it would provide a large amount of free heat to the hot-air engine, and the hot-air unit would be even more efficient than a modern automobile engine.

The principle of the hot-air engine is very old and should have been developed further. To understand it easily, suppose you take disks cut from a wire screen and place a stack of them inside a cylinder. Have the disks red hot at one end and progressively cooler towards the other. If you now push air back and forth through the disks, the air will be first hot and at high pressure, then cold and at low pressure. Every time the air is at the highest pressure, let it push a working piston down. When the air is at the lowest pressure, bring the piston back up.

To keep the screens from all becoming the same temperature there would need to be a heater at the hot end and a cooler at the other. An improved design for a hot-air engine would be as shown in Figure 30.

In the first drawing the air from the hot side must pass back through the heater as it pushes the piston down, which should help keep the pressure high for the entire stroke. One improvement is in the use of by-pass valves. Near the bottom of the

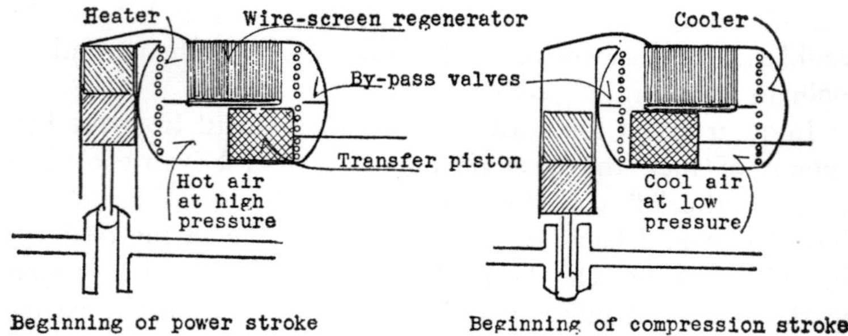

FIG. 30

stroke the by-pass valves should slide over first; then the transfer piston should move to the other end, as shown in the second drawing. As it does so, the air will by-pass the heater while it gives up heat first to the regenerator, then to the cooler. The power piston will then rise against low pressure. As it nears the top on its return stroke, the by-pass valves should change first; then as the transfer piston moves to the other end, it will cause the cool air to by-pass the cooler on its way to pick up heat from the regenerator and heater.

It has been found that a lightweight gas works better than air in such engines. The gas should be pumped in first to a high average pressure.

The hotter the gas is as it pushes the working piston down, the more efficient the engine will be. One way to use very hot gas is to make the working piston twice as tall as normal, the top half slightly smaller in diameter, so that it never quite touches the cylinder wall. The top half of both the cylinder and piston will never require any lubrication and may get as hot as they wish, if they are made out of the proper heat-resisting materials. The top half of the piston might even be insulated from the bottom half. This same type of construction would also work for a four-cycle Diesel and allow a much higher cylinder wall temperature for greater efficiency.

This design, however, would not work on a two-cycle Diesel,

because the piston must fit properly to cover the inlet ports until the time to uncover them. A two-cycle Diesel could be improved by using two exhaust valves for each cylinder, a high pressure valve to open at the normal time of about two-thirds of the way down, and a low pressure valve to open when the piston has nearly reached the bottom of the stroke. The high pressure exhaust would act as a jet pump placed in the low pressure exhaust of the cylinder that had last fired.

If the Diesel is a seven-cylinder radial and if the cylinder heads are laid out in a row, they would look like the ones in Figure 31.

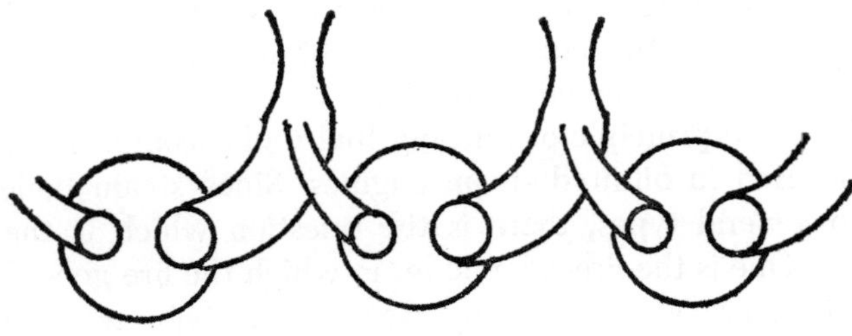

FIG. 31

In that way, the exhaust gas of each cylinder would be drawn out and fresh air pulled in without putting any load on the blower, which ordinarily absorbs horsepower from the crankshaft.

This same principle could be adapted to a four-cycle engine by using one large inlet and two exhaust valves. It would especially help a supercharged engine by cutting down the back pressure on the pistons.

For every dollar spent developing Diesel and gas engines, less than a penny has been spent on hot-air engines. Yet the hot-air engine can be more efficient, it can start under a heavy load without shifting gears, it is easily reversible, and it gives a clean exhaust.

If the object were to build a hot-air engine alone, rather than combining it with a gasoline or Diesel engine, a good design then would be a four-cylinder V-type. This design would allow all four heaters for the four cylinders to be so close together that just one burner could be used for all four.

The burner should consume the fuel under high compression. The compressor should be run by a compressed-air motor, and the compressed-air motor should operate on the exhaust from the burner, after it has gone through the heaters.

It should be possible for the heaters in the hot-air engine to lower the temperature of the gases passing through them to a certain point so that when the gases expand through the compressed-air motor, they will come out at about the same temperature as the air that was taken in by the compressor. Since the fuel enters as a liquid and comes out as a gas at much greater volume, the compressor might not absorb any power from the main engine while running.

This same principle of burning fuel under compression could also be used in oil-fired steam engines. Since steam boilers are of two general types, there is the question which is the more efficient. One is the fire-tube boiler in which the fire goes through tubes that are surrounded by water. This type was used for steam locomotives. The other is the water-tube boiler in which the water is inside the tubes and the fire outside.

As far as I know, the design that would produce the highest efficiency of all has never been tried. You would need two tubes, such as one of four inches, one of two inches. These should be turned into two separate coils exactly the same size when measured from the centers. The smaller coil should be screwed inside of the larger while both are upside down. When turned over, the smaller tube should rest on small fins welded every few feet along its side. These fins would hold the smaller tube in the center of the larger tube.

The fire should travel through the small tube while the water travels between the tubes. The fire and water should travel in opposite directions, so the water will come out at the hot end.

A coil only 12 feet in diameter and 12 feet high will contain about 1,000 feet of 4-inch tubing. The tubes should be at least that long. The main features of this system are shown in Figure 32.

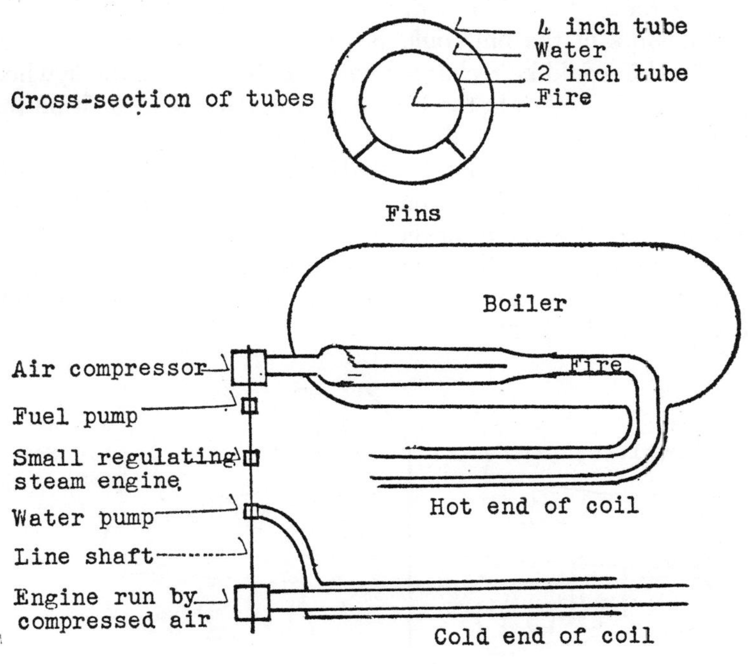

FIG. 32

If the air and fuel are burnt at the same pressure as the steam pressure, nothing would cause the 2-inch tube to collapse or explode, no matter how thin it is.

With proper design, the exhaust from the compressed-air engine could remain at the same temperature as when it entered the compressor. Fuel entering as a liquid and leaving as a gas may provide more than enough volume to run it. A carbonless fuel or a periodic puff of oxygen would keep it clean.

This same system for burning fuel while under compression could also be adapted to solid fuel such as coal or wood.

An airtight bin with a door on both top and bottom could be filled with fuel. After the air pressure inside the bin has been equalized with that of the fire, the bottom door could open. The fuel would fall into an elbow, with the fire burning at the bottom.

Before refilling the bin with fuel, the energy contained in the air pressure of the bin could be stored in a spinning flywheel, and the bin could be recharged with fuel in seconds, the flywheel pumping air back into the bin. Since the bin would then be full of fuel, it would not require so much air.

Practically all steam generated by modern boilers is used to drive turbines. Yet the turbine design that should be the most efficient has apparently never been tried. When a large volume of air under pressure is needed, as for a ship with gills along the bottom, a good design for a turbine and compressor combination is shown in Figure 33.

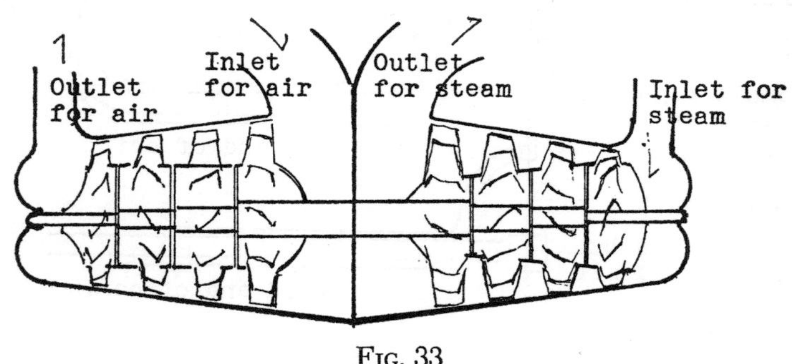

Fig. 33

The first and longest shaft is solid with bearings at each end. The next is hollow and just large enough to go over the first without touching it. It has ball bearings at each end and turns in the opposite direction. Each succeeding shaft goes over the one before it, and all have turbine blades on one end and compressor blades on the other. The partition in the center has such low pressure on each side that there would be no leakage.

Figure 33 shows the working principle. If high air compression is wanted, there could be additional compression stages.

The turbine part of this combination is more efficient than those now in use, because efficiency increases with speed, and centrifugal force limits the speed. By having alternate sets of blades turning in opposite directions, the relative speed would be twice as great. Each blade would fly like an airplane with a tail-wind. The compressor blades are also more efficient because of the angular direction of the air from the blades ahead.

To use this turbine design for other purposes, the compressor blades could be replaced with gears, with every other gear meshing with a gear on a separate shaft and the two separate shafts geared together.

The most efficient steam engine would look almost exactly like the hot-air engine. The steam would be heated for the power stroke and cooled for the compression stroke. When steam condenses, it gives up considerable heat that is normally wasted; but with this design the lost heat would be picked up again for the power stroke. No heat would be needed to continually evaporate fresh water as in present steam engines.

In the hot-air engine the high pressure is about three times greater than the low pressure, no matter what gases are used. The advantage of using steam instead of gas is that with the same increase in temperature steam would increase its pressure at a rate enormously greater.

One difference between a hot-air engine using steam and one using air or any other gas, would be in the cooling system. In a hot-air engine the cooler may remain exposed to the hot air, as very little air is affected. Where steam is used, however, the steam might continually condense against the cooler as the pressure tried to build up for the power stroke. To prevent this, the cooler could be completely covered with insulation each time the pressure is increased for the power stroke, and uncovered for the steam to go through the cooling fins to cause low pressure during the compression stroke, as in Figure 34.

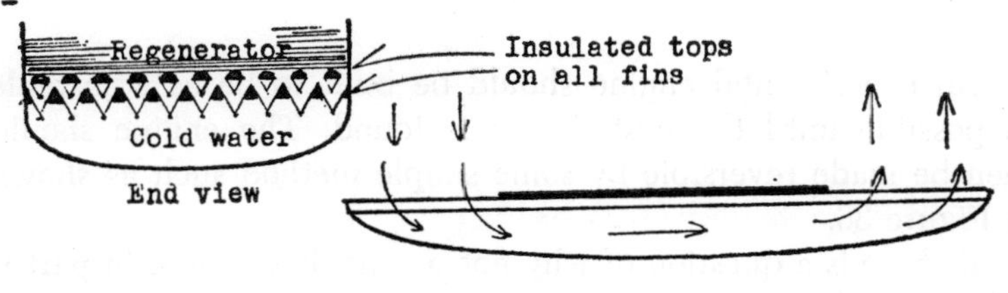

FIG. 34

The steam coming down through the regenerator would pass between each tapered fin. There it would move straight back to the other side, then up behind the transfer piston. When the steam was to be moved back, the movable fins would fit the stationary ones, so the steam would go directly to the regenerator, as in Figure 35.

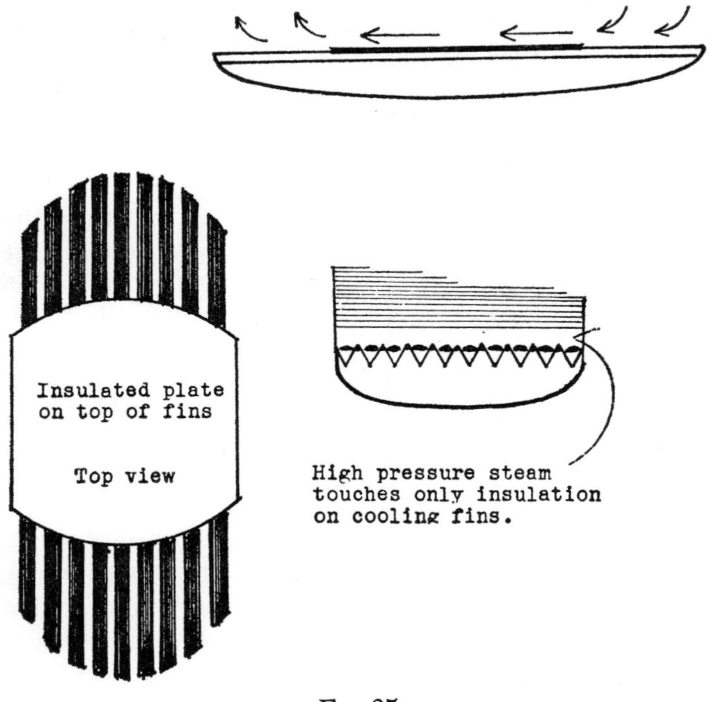

FIG. 35

An experimental engine should be built to be as adjustable as possible until the best design is found. The engine should then be made reversible by some simple method such as shown in Figure 36.

If there is a question of why not patent these ideas, in part it is because the patent system seems to me like tying up ideas so that no one else but their inventor can use them. Many people

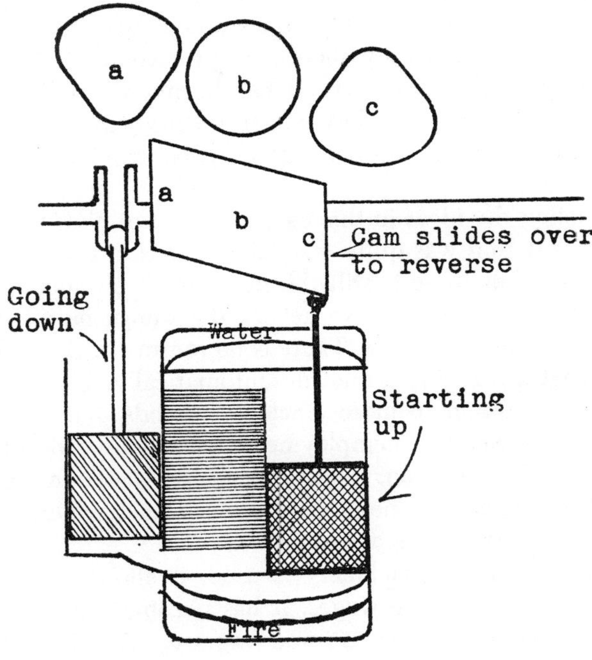

FIG. 36

have ideas for better and safer cars. Even a small boy knows that a big wheel rolls better than a small one, and all the other ideas in this chapter may have been thought of by some day-dreamer at some time or another, though I have never seen nor heard of these ideas before (except for the wall with strawberries growing from the side). Yet patents are granted on almost any kind of idea, provided it can be called both original and potentially useful.

The ideal patent system would not grant patents so easily, and it would allow any person to use any patent he wishes, provided he paid a fair price for any benefit he received. As it now exists, the patent system allows manufacturers who own a few vital patents to hold down competition. It also prevents many good inventions from being used. No patent system at all might be better for the country than what we now have.

Only a few inventions require so much expensive research and development that they should be protected. Multitudes of people can invent if they try. It has been estimated that the average patent holder has lost money on his patent, instead of making it. It is getting the idea into practical use that is difficult —and costly.

Concocting the ideas in this chapter was like playing a game requiring skill, and was quite enjoyable. Arriving at the finished design is fun, but there is still the problem of production.

For how each person is to get all the things he wants, the answer is simple in principle. There is no routine work performed by hand that a machine cannot do automatically. There is some organized opposition to more efficient methods, but machinery does not directly cause unemployment, for machines do not take money out of circulation, slow down its circulation, or raise wages. Only people do these things, any one of which will cut down the number of jobs available.

When laborsaving machinery is used, it allows for either a drop in prices or a rise in wages. It has become a policy in this country to use labor strikes to force wages up. An obvious argument against strikes is that usually more people are injured who are not involved in the dispute than in the dispute itself.

Another reason for not using force is even more important. If a person were completely selfish and knew what to do to get the most for himself, he would then do the same thing he would if he were trying to aim at the truth and obey the Ten Commandments. If a person believed he would live forever and that eternity would be better for himself if he did everything right and honestly, it would no longer be necessary to force him to do right. For these two reasons, no labor union has ever had a moral right to strike. Labor strife becomes more intense as pride becomes involved.

Concerning the more important problem of world peace, there can be no peace as long as pride is such a motivation in world affairs. Some reasons for war, such as freedom of the seas and boundary lines, are made to seem all-important by pride.

Line up the worldly reasons for war and place at the top of the list what feels the most important and all the rest in that order. If the most important reason could then be eliminated, everyone who deals with these problems would add some lesser reason to the bottom and move all the reasons up one place. That would happen each time the most important reason was eliminated. If all economic reasons for war could be eliminated, then some incident in Korea or Berlin would receive the same importance that any of the rest had ever received. For the feeling of importance is made strong by pride, and pride will always find a way to feel endangered.

It is interesting to see what the main features of a government would be if it could adopt an ideal economic system. An even bigger problem is how the morals of the people could be maintained at the highest level.

Eventually there will be an economic system that is more nearly ideal than our present one. It will still be a capitalistic system, but people will see money for what it really is. If money can't be understood any other way, it would be a good idea to have a statement printed on each piece of currency. One piece would say "one minute's work," one "five minutes' work," one "ten minutes' work," one "twenty-five minutes' work," one "fifty minutes' work," and one "one hundred minutes' work."

If prices fell so low because of laborsaving machinery that many small items would sell for less than a minute's worth of work, there could then be a coin minted for one-tenth of a minute's work.

If one man worked just one hour, he should receive two pieces of money; one would say "fifty minutes' work," the other, "ten minutes' work." If the work performed required previous training where he had to learn without being paid, he should be paid enough extra so that if he worked steadily for ten years, he would be paid in full. Should he quit before the ten years, he actually would have lost money in learning the job. Any time a person takes a chance on losing money, he is supposed to be taking a chance on making it, too. So, if he continues after the ten years he would be making a profit on his wages.

The length of time the average worker stays with a particular job after training should be considered, in determining the period for reimbursement. In any event, money should be considered as a medium of exchange that represents time at work, including time spent learning to perform the particular work.

If one man works one hour for you, you work one hour for him, and if you agree to trade even, then you both received the same wages. But if you can get him to work two hours for you in exchange for one hour of work that you do for him, you have now received a raise in wages. That is all that a higher wage really is.

However, higher-than-average wages are not good wages but unjust wages. When wages are understood as being unjust by those who forced them up, they must also be seen as dishonest. Fair wages are the best possible wages.

Each worker should be paid the same rate as everyone else, plus an additional amount for the cost of learning his job, when he learns on his own time. For added risk or expensive tools that a worker must furnish, there should be adequate pay. The cost of training should be determined by the amount of time it takes the average worker to learn the job, as well as any money he must spend to learn it.

If your job requires you to read and write, you should not receive extra pay for knowing something that everyone must learn anyway for his own welfare.

The problem of fair profits is different. You might use the savings of a lifetime to start a business and lose it in a short time. That would be fair enough, for that is the chance that was taken. If you can lose it in six months, however, you should also have a chance to double it in that time. If you succeed in doubling your money and reinvest it in your own business, it can produce a snowballing effect.

If you double your money and reinvest it successfully, you might soon be making a million dollars a year. This is all right if there is no price fixing and competition remains fair. To keep competition fair, one manufacturer should not be allowed to pay lower wages than another, and he should not be allowed to bribe workers to work in his factory by paying higher wages. Wages should remain fixed while the living standard should rise in the form of lower prices.

Lower prices would be brought about by laborsaving methods. A fair return to those responsible for any new laborsaving method might be one-third of what it saves over a one-year period. The way to rapid industrial progress is to pay an employee well for any idea or invention that he contributes, if it helps do the work any faster, better, or safer.

There might be two factories side by side, both manufacturing the same product. One could be losing money, even though all of its employees are working as diligently as they can with out-of-date methods. The other factory could be making very large profits, even though all of its workers have easy jobs and sit down at automatic machines. The workers with the soft jobs should not receive higher wages just because the company they work for is making larger profits. There should be no profit sharing, for all wages are entirely relative to other wages, never to profits.

If a business or industry does make very large profits, the most good it can do with the money would be to spend it on research and development. The next most good would be to lower the price of the products it sells; the next, to distribute the money to the stockholders and call it profits. The entire industrial machine should be considered as a large game, a game that anyone may try to play. It can be fun to run things, but whether you try to reach an executive position in a large company or start a small one and expand it with its own earnings, the name of the game is profits. The government should be the referee and see to it that there are no price fixing, no trusts, and no spiraling wage rates.

The only difference between average wages of ten dollars a day and average wages of one million dollars is one of degree. Another name for high wages is inflation, and another name for inflation is high wages.

If wages were controlled, along with the total amount of money in the nation, and if the speed of circulation remained normal, the nation could then take its choice in any degree between having a shortage of workers, with a large number of jobs available, or a shortage of jobs, so that manufacturers could choose from a large number of workers when hiring.

With the first choice would go a tight supply of goods. With the second would go unemployment, with its attendant welfare problem.

The best would be the first choice with the shortage of workers. A manufacturer might employ a hiring agent to go to the home of a nonworker in an attempt to persuade that person to come work for him. Factory managers could organize social clubs for their own employees as one inducement. Another inducement would be to have half the jobs performed standing up, and half sitting down. Each worker would then learn two jobs so that he could alternate standing with sitting.

To continually maintain more jobs than workers, each person should cooperate in controlling the speed of circulation. If the government estimated a need for ten percent more jobs, the information should be told to the nation with the request that each person should hold his income for a ten percent shorter time after he earns it. If the average speed of circulation increased ten percent, that would put ten percent more people to work.

If the government judged that a shortage of goods was getting too severe, it should request that each person hold his money longer before buying. Getting public cooperation might be difficult, especially in holding down the wage scale.

With many more jobs available than there are workers, there should be no opposition to operating prisons as factories. A prisoner might be sentenced to perform a certain amount of work. If he put in full time working, he would be released sooner. A prisoner who refused to work would be sentencing himself to life imprisonment.

Prison factories would save tax dollars. Even more important than money, the prisoners would acquire the habit of doing useful work; a big help after their release.

Prisoners who wished to learn a profession should be allowed to do so. In cases where a prisoner already had a profession, he might work as a teacher for others. They should all be under Social Security for a pension.

Old-age pensions paid for by any business or industry should be outlawed, for two reasons. One is that the pensions are really paid for by the ultimate consumer. Since everyone pays, everyone should receive. A government pension to the aged is better. The other reason why industrial pensions should be eliminated, or at least kept very small, is that no industry can afford to hire an older worker when it must very soon retire him on a pension. The most justification for industrial pensions is that some workers would too readily quit their jobs, if it were not for losing their pensions.

In putting the right policies into practice the electing of the right candidates to office is more important than the parties they represent. But there are two reasons why the two-party system of selecting candidates is still the best. One is that dividing a large number of candidates into two opposing camps will cause many people to become more interested because of the game-spirit involved. Everybody likes a game. Anything that makes people become more interested in their government is a help.

Another reason is that each party tries to keep its own house in order and the criminal element out. If it were not for this close scrutiny from one's own party, a time might come when outright criminals would run for office for the sole purpose of funneling public funds into their own pockets.

As long as so many people lean towards dishonesty, it will be necessary to have many safeguards for keeping criminals out of office.

Probably the biggest disgrace in our form of government today is the filibuster. Important legislation has often had to wait for a filibuster to end, and it may last until Congress adjourns. If the majority thinks a proposal is undesirable, it should be put to a vote so that the majority can turn it down.

If human nature were good enough to permit the best system for electing candidates, the machinery for such a system would be much simpler than at present. The best system would allow any would-be candidate to run for any national office. To run for president, the candidate would need to get a certain number of names on a petition from his home town. He would then debate publicly with any rival candidate from the same town, and the cost would be paid for by that town. The voters would select the winner in a local election. The winner would proceed to the next largest district, where the winners from all the cities in that district would debate the issues. At each level the debates, and the election itself, would be paid for by the people of that town, district, or state. It would end with the government paying for the last series of debates, and the final election.

Each voter would list all candidates in order of his preference, to the end of the list if he wished. In counting the votes, the candidate with the least votes would be eliminated first. Voters who voted for him would have their second choice moved up to first place and the votes again counted. The candidate with the least votes would again be eliminated. This would continue until only the winner would remain. In that way no candidate would be splitting the vote for any other.

The voting could be done by machine, and with each voter voting for all candidates at one time only one voting period would be necessary in the finals, no matter how many candidates were running for office.

The greatest improvement in this world will have to come through an improvement in human nature. In the early 1930s there was speculation in my town about a small item in the local newspaper stating that Nostradamus predicted that at that time a world-shaking event would take place, but it would go largely unnoticed. It was at that time Lucifer quit thinking he was good. Until then, when any person thought of himself as being good, the thought would cause a strong feeling of pride. When a person now tries to act good and think of himself as good, it will cause no direct feeling of pride, only an inherited feeling of it, which makes it seem phony. As a result, the world lost a strong feeling that formerly helped people to behave themselves.

The Bible says that the end of this world shall be preceded by a great apostasy, that there will come a falling away, that iniquity shall abound. There has been a relatively sudden change recently in sex morals, in religious faith, and in nearly all types of crime. One of the main reasons for this condition has been the loss of pride in being good. Pride, though, has never been the right motive for proper behavior; although it has been a very strong one.

The most practical way to improve human nature is to teach each person before he is five years old the reasons why he should be honest and behave himself, as well as the reasons why he should not be dishonest or misbehave; also, why proper behavior is so difficult. Each one inherits many different paths of behavior. Some paths are desirable, some are undesirable. Some paths are wide, some are narrow. If a person has parents and grandparents who are dishonest, he will inherit a wide path tending towards dishonest behavior. If he is made aware that he has such paths in his own mind, it will be that much easier to avoid them. In whichever direction a person starts, he has a strong tendency to keep going.

Some of the widest paths concern sexual behavior. What is needed here is the right answers to questions asked by the very young. Even without any sexual training, the majority reach the teen years without much serious trouble. However, before they reach twenty they will meet with situations for which they must already know the answers, for they will not have time to think.

Young people first should know some very simple facts. There are physical, emotional, and spiritual reasons why it is better for a person not to have sexual intercourse until he gets married, and then only with his spouse.

The physical reasons are the most preventable. They include venereal disease, and for girls the possibility of pregnancy and various forms of physical injury. When prostitutes are involved, money might be considered as something physical. Venereal disease is sometimes contracted even though prophylactics are used. So, physical reasons should not be minimized.

The emotional reasons are more or less unavoidable. Anything that interferes with happiness can be called an emotional reason.

Another reason in the unhappy class is gossip. It is practically impossible to keep fornication a secret, even from members of your own family. A much more important emotional reason for behaving yourself is that you probably have strong ideals concerning marriage. Even if not, we all have ancestors who thought it was a good idea to be married. So we have inherited marital ideals.

Anything that undermines your ideals will interfere with your happiness. Prostitution interferes with the ideals of marriage to a very great degree. Since you had many kinds of ancestors with all kinds of ideals, both high and low, you have inherited many different kinds of instincts and you must consciously discriminate amongst them.

Each male has an instinct that makes him look down on any female with whom he has had sexual intercourse, if he is not married to her. This instinct may be either strong or weak depending on the character of his ancestors and his own parents, as well as on character traits he has developed in his own early life.

Even when this instinct is very weak, it is better to avoid its influence altogether by waiting until after marriage before beginning sexual relations. Some men will not marry one they look down upon. In some cases the couple has sexual intercourse with the full intention of getting married later on, but then they drift apart. If they had waited, they would have gotten married with a good chance for happiness.

In an ideal marriage the husband and wife should feel that their partners are their best friends. This relationship is interfered with when you have to lie to your best friend.

The sexual side of life can also act as a foundation that will support a great amount of additional feelings. An analogy is when a man liked to fish, and because of that he built a motorboat that not only afforded him much satisfaction and pleasure while building it, but later derived considerable happiness from operating the boat. In fact, he would not have built the boat if he had not liked to fish. In this case, the fishing acted as a foundation.

The ones with high morals have a freshness about them. But when they try everything to excess they have jaded feelings.

Side issues, such as nudity or semi-nudity in public should also have answers based on logic. If everyone went naked, in time it would kill off sex desire almost completely. If the opposite were tried and the women wore veils over their faces, as was done in Turkey for centuries, it would eventually produce the opposite effect. In that event, just to see a naked face would be very exciting. A sensible compromise is the answer.

The spiritual reasons for behaving are the most important. When a virgin of either sex commits adultery with a person who is motivated by demon feelings, it will produce a strong feeling of being dirty. Most spiritual reasons will hinge on the fact that when you die, it is just your body that dies. Your personality will still need to be perfected. If you have had sexual relations with a prostitute, you will have to overcome the instinct that makes you look down on her.

This will be brought about by having the plans of the world run over again the same way. It will look and seem the same, but you will be the only one in the world who is real. All the rest of the people will be just plans. Also, you will not be the same fellow you are now, for you must be each prostitute with whom you have had sexual intercourse.

If you have had sex relations with a dozen prostitutes, the life of each one will have to be run over just for you; or at least for that part of her life that you must understand. The reason is that all women are born with an instinct against prostitution. There are no born prostitutes, so it has to be somebody else's fault each time a girl becomes one.

After you have become each of the prostitutes, you will no longer be able to look down on any of them. The reason you will have to be each one is for education only, not for punishment.

There is no punishment for its own sake. Eternity has been planned to produce the most happiness from all sources, including marriage.

As for maintaining the moral behavior of each person during his lifetime at high levels, this could be done by his learning the reasons why it is better for himself if he behaves, and then learning them, before he starts on the wrong paths. Some will do better if they have a very high and unselfish motive. The upper limit in this direction is trying to think what God would say do.

Even a small thing that is undesirable, such as swearing, will have adequate reasons for its prohibition. There are professional violin players who cannot play quite as well as they might have played, because when they were very young they heard someone use "fiddlesticks" as a cuss word. When anything bad enough happens suddenly, it will cause a feeling of dislike, and any word you use to swear with will get the feeling connected to it. This principle is especially strong where names are used for swearing, as swearing changes the meaning and feelings associated with the names. Some would say that swearing blunts the finer things. Also, your audience will either dislike your swearing or imitate it.

The effect of connecting undesirable feelings to a subject has been demonstrated in many unhappy marriages. Psychiatrists have found that lewdness in sexy jokes and stories become connected to the subject of sex, and the feelings are then carried over into the sexual side of marriage, making an ideal sex life impossible. Platonic love and lewdness are incompatible.

Many years ago I attended some lectures by a doctor who explained how people can be unduly influenced by any subject they think about when they dwell on it too much. The example he gave was that of a preacher who tried to rob a bank, because he had become obsessed with detective stories and read them incessantly. I have noticed ever since how easily people are influenced by repeated impressions. The abundance of crime, violence, and sex shown on television and in the movies has been more influential on our national behavior than most people think. The negative side will have to be eliminated before people will be able to conduct themselves well.

When everyone knows the reasons for better behavior, it will not only be possible to have good conduct but would be possible to disseminate birth control information without the fear that it would lower moral standards. For birth control is more desirable than most people realize.

Birth control may be the only hope for preventing starvation in India, China, and elsewhere, but there are other advantageous reasons people may not yet see. People in many small towns will believe that with more people coming into their hamlets to live and pay taxes, taxes will be lower. But there is an absolute limit to how low taxes can get in a normal American town and still provide the services and facilities the citizens demand.

If a town has just the right size schoolhouse, police force, water mains, sewers, other utilities, and paved streets, that state of affairs will allow the lowest possible taxes. An increase in population must then necessitate enlarging all services, with much higher taxes for each taxpayer. Cities that are continually growing, like New York City, are famous for high taxes.

Another problem that plagues the big city is the racial problem. This is next in importance to a third world war. There is the question of how conflicts and strife, such as the Vietnam war and the racial problem, should be handled. Anyone who believes he can feel the truth should enjoy trying to cope with these two problems.

22

Education and International Problems

Education can be vastly improved by better teaching methods. Much depends on reading ability. Some teachers argue in favor of the phonetic method of reading, some for the sight method. The right way is to teach both to complement each other.

Instead of reading stories from a book to the pupils in the elementary grades, each teacher should read from a screen on which stories are printed. A mechanical hand should point to each word, and the pupils should sit where they can see each word as they learn its meaning. In this way the meaning of each word becomes associated with the way it looks. After learning in this manner, it is easy to read several times faster than you can talk and still comprehend every word.

Next, the alphabet should be taught along with the sound of each letter. Words can then be looked up in a dictionary, and words that are spelled nearly the same can be told apart.

If you must change the written word into a sound, the sound into its meaning, you are a slow reader. But if you can count to ten over and over again out loud while reading to yourself, you are on the right track. It is easier to learn to read fast by the sight method than it is to learn to read slow by the phonetic method; but if you learn the slow way first you get stuck in the habit.

Writing by hand can be greatly facilitated by having a special holder with a pencil clamped at one end and the other end strapped to the arm. There should be one of these devices for each pupil in the first grade. It would then be impossible to use a finger motion in writing. After the pupil acquires a strong habit of using the proper arm motion for writing, the holder can be dispensed with.

By the time a child is old enough to begin school, it may be too late for him to learn the best way to use numbers. Numbers should be thought of as amounts, instead of the way they look or sound. It is possible to add, subtract, multiply, and divide without knowing how to either write a digit or say it. Some people can solve arithmetic problems involving large sums mentally and rapidly.

Some of these geniuses would have been ordinary in arithmetic, but at an early age, before they learned to count or write numbers, they played with objects such as rocks or marbles, arranging them like spots on playing cards. After making up their minds to think of numbers as amounts and becoming proficient in their use, it was then proper to learn to write numbers and pronounce them.

If a successful character-building program instilling honesty could be used for the very young, it would do more good than improving the three "R's."

Games could be devised that would be highly educational. Elementary economics could be taught to the very young through games involving money. They would learn that if all wages in the United States came down to one dollar a day, there would not be a single nickel that would disappear into thin air; there would still be as much money as before.

Each time money is spent, the new owner of it has the right to spend it. If each person held his money for a long time before spending it, that would be a slow speed of circulation. If each one spent it as soon as he could, that would be a very fast speed of circulation. Every time a day's wages were spent, that would create another day's work, if wages did not rise.

They would learn further that there is no limit to how high wages can go; there is no point where it is good wages on one side but inflation on the other.

Games involving character building are especially desirable. Also literature of that type, of which there is a much larger choice. There have been many changes in the past that have been undesirable. Progress means change, but change does not necessarily mean progress.

It could be seriously argued that it doesn't matter much any more how the young are trained, because of the type of weapons that are now in production, and how a small war may escalate.

The Vietnam-type of war may arise again in the future, so a study of the cause and cure should be profitable. The right plan for the Vietnam-type of problem can be found by a look at history. The United States was having the same problem that Japan had in China.

In the early 1930s Japan tried a coprosperity plan. When Japan invaded China to make China an industrial nation, Japan made the mistake of trying to conquer all of China before it industrialized any of it. What it should have done was present a cooperative plan that would appeal to China, and then take only as much as it could completely control and modernize.

With Japan supervising the industry and trading for the finished products, the Chinese in this area would be far richer than the average and would enjoy a much higher living standard. The Chinese people of the surrounding area would have welcomed industrial expansion when they could see it as an advantage. It would be an ever-widening circle of influence for the Japanese. It had to be either cooperation or failure.

It was the same situation in Vietnam, cooperation or failure. The reason for our going into Vietnam can be stated in a broad sense by saying that it was to do the most good for the Vietnamese people. It is possible for the United States to help the people set up a government where free and fair elections could decide who would win in each election.

When a nation is under communism, the means of production are owned by the people in common, instead of by individuals, as in capitalism. It is doubtful if many Vietnamese people on either side of the war know much about communism or care about it. The enemy soldiers do not need communism to fight for. All they need is something to fight against.

To help keep the peace in any other nation, we should never

spend money on offensive warfare. If the same amount of money were spent on civilian improvements, a good example could be made of that part of a nation where we have the cooperation of the people, and then every effort made to win over the rest to the same way of living.

Getting the people to cooperate over a gradually widening area should be our main effort. When we use military means, this raises a vast amount of resistance. Japan ran into so much resistance in China that she was stalled for ten years before the United States entered the war.

The bombing of Pearl Harbor seemed so unexpected that many people may not know what led to it. What did was our participating in the conflict the same way other nations could get involved with us in the future. A review of events that led to the bombing of our bases might help understand this type of situation.

The bombing of Pearl Harbor was caused by a series of mistakes; China made the first. Japan then made the second, China made the third, the United States made the fourth—and the next was the bombing of Pearl Harbor. China had much raw material that was not being used. Japan's idea was to develop this raw material, in cooperation with China, to their mutual benefit.

But China turned down the proposition. Japan made the second mistake by invading China and trying to force the plan into operation. After the invasion, China made the third mistake by resisting it with force.

After ten years of such fighting, the United States made the mistake of "laying down the law" to Japan and demanding that Japan retreat all the way to its own shoreline. All negotiations broke down over our insistence that Japan give up all it had gained.

We were using considerable economic pressure against Japan and we did have an aid-to-China policy which we could greatly increase. The Japanese could have stopped our ships with their navy, but that would have meant war. It would be to their advantage to make it a surprise attack.

If the United States would have nothing to do with offensive warfare, there would be no strong appeal to patriotism among the natives to drive out an invader. All of our initiative from now on should be towards civilian prosperity. Enemy infiltration should be dealt with by the natives.

Only the most fundamental principles of the main problems can be stated here. The spiritual side, which means the way it effects eternity, is most important. The spiritual side is a happy side. The most important questions in this life are of a spiritual nature, and they are the aim and purpose of this book.

23

Purpose of This Book

Any way of helping the general welfare was desired, but more specifically the purpose of this book concerns eternity. Mark 8:36, says, "For what shall it profit a man, if he should gain the whole world, and lose his own soul?" The Bible states that you are saved by faith. With faith so important, the question arises of how to acquire faith. Heb. 11:1, says, "Now faith is the substance of things hoped for, the evidence of things not seen." Presenting a picture of the things hoped for and the evidence for it should help in acquiring faith.

A summary of the reasons why the hereafter will be much better than now would include the following:

1. Everything good that happens to you will be compared to something very much worse, contained in the Lord's House instead of the Heart of Man.

2. The physical reality of the world will be made of feelings that are all good instead of half good and half bad, that make the neutral reality of the present.

3. With all old instincts done away with and a fresh start made at building up new ones of feelings that are all good, the new Heart of Man will eventually become the most important factor in making eternity good.

4. All present-day skills will be had by each person, plus the right to get more if he has the ticket for them.

5. There will be the absence of all negative qualities. Besides the beauty shop team there are others. Everything worth having has been paid for, including perfect health.

6. There will be more kinds of desirable feelings than at present.

7. Other people's feelings create a spirit that you can pick

up and feel, too. For eternity your happiness will allow you to enter the spirit of happiness from the rest of the world.

8. There will be sources of spiritual knowledge for each one that are unavailable now.

9. Each one will feel three times more alive than he does now.

10. Marriages will be much happier for many reasons. After several lifetimes have gone by on this world there will be inherited memories that will make a husband think his wife seems like a part of himself and vice versa. They will be more like one.

11. There will be certain spiritual changes which are hardly imagined now, such as having the bottom of the first heaven attainable.

12. There will be no Death or Hell when it comes time to leave this world.

When you leave this present life the one responsible for your safety is Emmanuel, so it is better if you form an opinion of him. Some argue that Emmanuel is God in the flesh.

Yet I believe that Emmanuel, while in this world, was a normal man, except that he had no interference between himself and the Holy Spirit, because he really had a virgin birth. So, there was no interference caused by instincts from a long line of male ancestors. And because he could see the knowledge of the Holy Spirit, which includes all fundamental knowledge, he could easily see how to accomplish all of the miracles that were reported of him.

Under the same circumstances, you also could perform miracles with all knowledge. If you then stepped over on the Holy Spirit side to speak, you would be speaking as God. In other words, you are also God, but there is so much interference between your consciousness and God that you are unaware of it.

In overcoming death, Emmanuel received the spiritual right to bring forth everyone else who is in death anytime he wishes. The name Christ is the name of a position. It is from the words "cry first." Emmanuel was the first to be heard through the spirit of this world, which is death. The feelings he sustained while on the cross had to last only six hours to be able to support all profit feelings. That is because of the four periods in each day which are continually repeated.

A statement in the Bible that is very hard to understand is John 1:29. Here it states that Emmanuel will take away the sin of the world. Many people have wondered how Emmanuel could take away their sins or those of anyone else. The way is for Emmanuel to use all the trouble the sins have caused, which changes them from what they are to something useful and necessary for making eternity very enjoyable. All evil can be turned to good, even the vinegar Emmanuel was given to drink. Before Emmanuel can use your troubles for eternity, you must be there, too.

Emmanuel also has the very high position of being one of the trinity which forms the head of your entire being. This trinity is called a soul. For the three parts of his own soul one function is performed by the Holy Ghost, one by the Spirit of Love, and the other one he does himself. As the Spirit of Truth, he is involved in everything that happens. An inventor discovers his own invention while Emmanuel looks at it. As far as the entire universe is concerned, God creates, Emmanuel looks at it, and everyone else discovers.

Everyone will be familiar with the Spirit of Truth for eternity, which will eliminate the present-day confusion of not knowing what to do. With all people having a knowledge of the truth firsthand they will not have to be telling each other about it.

This is stated in Heb. 8:10,11: "For this is the covenant that I will make with the house of Israel after those days, saith the Lord; I will put my laws into their mind, and write them in their hearts: and I will be to them a God, and they shall be to me a people.

"And they shall not teach every man his neighbour, and every man his brother, saying, Know the Lord: for all shall know me, from the least to the greatest."

To "Know the Lord" will mean increased ability as well as knowledge. For the Spirit of Truth is the Lord of everything that happens. As for any person receiving any honor for his accomplishments, it will someday be understood that all real honor comes from God and that it is a form of ambition.

If you try to help others and if your efforts causes them enjoyment or helps them in any way, it is not necessary for them to know that it was you who did it. And it is not necessary for you to know that anyone liked what you did. But the Holy Spirit does use the help or enjoyment you gave to others to give you honor. The amount of honor he gives you depends on the strength of your motives and how well the people liked what you did.

Young children often display the right motives. If the world were motivated by that kind of honor now, it would be called sweet. But now the world is running on such as vinegar.